# The Language of Lies

# The Language of Lies
*How to Uncover the Liar in Your Life*

KIRSTY KING

**Cornerstone Press**

CORNERSTONE PRESS

UK | USA | Canada | Ireland | Australia
India | New Zealand | South Africa

Cornerstone Press is part of the Penguin Random House group of companies whose addresses can be found at global.penguinrandomhouse.com

Penguin Random House UK,
One Embassy Gardens, 8 Viaduct Gardens, London SW11 7BW

penguin.co.uk

First published 2026

001

Copyright © Kirsty King, 2026

The moral right of the author has been asserted

Penguin Random House values and supports copyright. Copyright fuels creativity, encourages diverse voices, promotes freedom of expression and supports a vibrant culture. Thank you for purchasing an authorised edition of this book and for respecting intellectual property laws by not reproducing, scanning or distributing any part of it by any means without permission. You are supporting authors and enabling Penguin Random House to continue to publish books for everyone. No part of this book may be used or reproduced in any manner for the purpose of training artificial intelligence technologies or systems. In accordance with Article 4(3) of the DSM Directive 2019/790, Penguin Random House expressly reserves this work from the text and data mining exception.

Set in 12.9/16.2pt Dante MT Pro
Typeset by Six Red Marbles UK, Thetford, Norfolk

Printed and bound in Great Britain by Clays Ltd, Elcograf S.p.A.

The authorised representative in the EEA is Penguin Random House Ireland, Morrison Chambers, 32 Nassau Street, Dublin D02 YH68

A CIP catalogue record for this book is available from the British Library

ISBN: 978–1–529–95964–2

Penguin Random House is committed to a sustainable future for our business, our readers and our planet. This book is made from Forest Stewardship Council® certified paper.

For my mother and brother

# Contents

*Introduction*     1

1. Words: How to detect lexical lies     17
2. Grammar: How to detect lies of little changes     68
3. Paraverbal: How to detect lies in vocal cues     111
4. Prepare: How to get ready for linguistic lie detection     147

*Conclusion*     181

*Acknowledgements*     185

*Notes*     187

# Introduction

It was around Christmas time some years ago, when someone very close to me, let's call him Caleb, returned home early from work clearly in shock. He slowly and haltingly recounted what had happened when he arrived at his shift that morning: the police had been waiting for him. They took him into a room and without any warning, one of the police officers told him bluntly that his girlfriend was dead and asked him: 'What do you know about it?'

Caleb and his girlfriend had met at work. They were both in their early twenties and they had begun seeing each other a few months after first meeting. She'd had a previous boyfriend; they had been engaged but she had broken it off. By the time she met Caleb she had moved out of the flat she had shared with her ex-fiancé.

Just before Christmas, Caleb and his girlfriend went out after work for an evening meal together. Quietly, she confided in him how scared she was of her ex-fiancé. He was violent, manipulative and possessive. After she had broken off their engagement, she'd had to leave the small flat they shared even though it was hers. She was happy to be out of such an abusive relationship, but her happiness was mixed with fear that her ex would find out she was dating someone new and cause problems. She and Caleb agreed that they would not meet up in her home town where her ex lived, which was about half an hour's drive away, so as not to risk running into him.

It was dark by the time they finished their meal and Caleb walked her back to her car which was parked outside their workplace. Standing by her car, they chatted and hugged and he gave her a present. She wanted to give Caleb a lift home, but he wouldn't let her: it was late, so he told her to get home safe, he was fine to walk home and he would see her in the morning at their shift. They kissed goodbye, she got in her car and Caleb watched as she drove away.

He would never see her again.

Neither she nor Caleb saw the man hiding in the back of her car. Her ex-fiancé had followed her to work, broken into her car, and waited for her. He saw Caleb and her together, he saw the present, he saw them kiss. He waited until she had driven far enough away, before creeping out of the back and forcing her to drive to the flat they had once shared together. As soon as he got her inside the flat, he brutally attacked her. Using a weapon, he repeatedly hit her until she was unconscious, bleeding and barely alive. Then he calmly swallowed a box of paracetamol and phoned for an ambulance.

When the medics and police arrived, Caleb's girlfriend

## INTRODUCTION

was dead. Her ex lied to them, saying it had been a suicide pact gone wrong. He was taken to hospital and treated for his overdose. He survived.

Unbelievably, the police pursued their investigation into the circumstances of her death as a suicide pact. As part of their procedure, they wanted to speak to her work colleagues, including Caleb, to see if she'd had any reason to want to end her life. Caleb's evidence of what she had revealed about her ex-fiancé forced the police to pursue a murder charge against her killer instead. At the trial, it was Caleb's word against the ex-fiancé's. The trial ended with a murder conviction. Sentenced to life in prison, this abusive man nearly got away with murdering a young woman by telling a simple lie.

Sometimes we don't realise the moments in our lives that set us on a particular path to our future selves. I often think it was this moment – learning that the police could believe such an outrageous lie that would allow a killer to get away with murder – that set me on the path to study language and linguistics.

For over twenty years, I have been researching and lecturing in linguistics. Linguists study language, although we are commonly misunderstood to be speakers of many languages: polyglots. What linguists in fact do is uncover and investigate the mysteries of language; we search for the unconscious knowledge that humans have about the way we communicate. We analyse language so we can offer insight into the human mind. We investigate how languages are organised, how they are structured and how they are used. We analyse the sounds, the words and the sentences, their meanings, patterns and combinations, along with how we all physically produce language, and how we and others perceive or understand language. It is a fascinating field that intersects with almost every other discipline such as psychology, sociology, anthropology and history.

My research covers quite a few areas and one of these is deceptive language use. This focuses on analysing the language use of speakers who claim they are someone else. My research into these claims covers the fields of forensic linguistics (language and the law),[1] conversation analysis (social interaction) and pragmatics (language in use) in order to analyse the language of these speakers to find out if they really are who they say they are.

The language that we all use exposes so much about us, including that which we think we can hide – like the truth or who we really are.

Let me explain this a bit more for you. As soon as someone speaks, we might identify that person's educational and economic background, their social class, or their place of upbringing. This ability to detect the hidden significance of language comes naturally to us all. We are hard-wired and attuned to identify so much about a person just from the way they speak.

It is not only a speaker's socio-economic status that

is revealed in their language use, however, but also things like specific personality types, mood and psychiatric disorders. Different personality types use language in different ways.[2] For example, individuals who have a neurotic personality display high emotional reactivity, whereby small things trigger an extreme reaction. These individuals will display moody behaviour and are more likely to be anxious, angry, frustrated, envious and depressive. Their language will use high-immediacy words such as first-person pronouns (I, my), and will contain more negative emotion words (futile, low, worry, sad), rather than positive emotion words (grateful, happy, hopeful, amused). Their particular language use is because neurotic personality types are worriers who are self-preoccupied. This focus on their self is mapped to their language use with their high use of first-person pronouns, and their worrying is evidenced in their use of more negative emotion words.

People who have a clear self-absorbed focus are considered to have a narcissistic personality and might be assumed to use the first-person pronoun (I) much more than people without this personality trait. However, this is an assumption likely based upon others' perception of narcissists.[3] In fact, high occurrences of first-person pronoun use are found in depressed, as opposed to non-depressed, individuals. Just like neurotics, this high occurrence is probably due to the self-focus that those with depression also have. This type of language use can be a diagnostic tool. The rate of occurrence of first-person pronouns in the speech of individuals appears to be a better indicator of depression than the use or occurrence of negative emotion words.[4]

So linguistic analysis of language can identify patterns in the speech of people with different types of personality, and in individuals with certain psychiatric conditions such as schizophrenia. In these individuals, it appears that there is a higher use of third-person pronouns (he, she, they) and fewer first-person singular pronouns (I) than individuals presenting with mood disorders.[5] The higher use of the third-person pronouns is suggested as being due to a decreased focus on the self, or that typically in schizophrenia the self is considered as the 'other', which is the third person. What is remarkable is that language can reveal an individual's focus and this appears to be a strong factor in determining a higher use of particular pronouns.

As language use can be a tool to support the diagnosis of specific personality types and disorders, along with revealing age, gender and even identity, we should therefore expect that language can reveal the difference between truth-tellers and liars as well. And this is exactly what we do find.

The evidence presented in this book is drawn from scientific studies from linguistics and psychology into the verbal cues of deception. Many of these studies use experimental methods such as constructing an artificial scenario where participants engage in some form of deception or lying task. These tasks allow the researchers to identify particular forms of language use that arise more commonly when the participants are being untruthful or deceitful. Other studies have used an alternative method to approach the discovery of linguistic cues to deception: examining a corpus of spoken language. The corpus studies have collected data from naturally occurring language to identify higher occurrences of certain linguistic forms (words, grammar, paraverbal) which arise in the language of liars. Some of these corpus studies are inspired by the results of the experimental methods studies and support the findings of the artificial scenarios with real-life data.

Throughout this book, the results of the studies are presented and illustrated with narratives which exemplify the use of particular linguistic cues to lying and deceit. Many of these narratives, accounts, transcripts, dialogues, interviews and stories are taken from documented real-life cases I have drawn together from many hours of video, audio and transcript analysis of speakers who are being deceptive – including some well-known ones. The cases presented throughout the book have been transcribed to detail where any pauses or fillers such as 'um' or 'er' appear in the speakers' language. I have used a form of transcription which includes three-point ellipses to show when the speakers have paused. When the pauses are of a longer length I have also shown this with [pause] and with specifying the timing. There are a few cases where fillers are used by speakers who do not pause before or after using them, and so no ellipsis is included. These speakers' deception and lying is confirmed by their conviction of a crime, evidence or confession. I have also included a few from my own experience in encountering liars as well.

Many of the cases presented come from situations of 'high-stakes' lying. This is where a liar can face serious risk if their lies are not believed, such as in cases of murder, robbery, adultery and fraud. These instances offer you a clear insight into how a lying speaker uses certain types of language (whether consciously or unconsciously) which give research-backed indications that what they are saying is likely to be untrue in some way.

We will also look at examples of more 'low-stakes' lying and deception, such as those from work colleagues, partners, politicians and journalists. These are more everyday instances where the risks to the liar are not that serious and there is reduced harm in their lies being believed. The linguistic cues to deception in these cases can sometimes be harder to detect than our high-stakes liars, although with researchers collecting more naturalistic language data from spontaneous speech and discourse, our understanding of verbal lie detection in these everyday cases will increase.

There are many types of lies, and there are many variations on their strength and the intent behind them. Lies

## INTRODUCTION

can be separated into fibs (little lies) and whoppers (big lies). We can specify the impact that certain lies have on others – to libel someone may be worse than to mislead them, but to slander someone is pretty bad. The English language can specify the size of a lie, whether the lie has malicious intent or implications, whether the lie is told to manipulate someone, and even whether the lie is a criminal offence (perjury). Differentiating between lies is very important. When we depart from the truth, we need words to show how we have departed from the truth, to what extent we have departed from it and the importance or gravity that the lie has on someone, a situation or something. In English, the reason we have such a high number of words for lying is because all these variations are necessary to serve our communicative needs. We need to be able to make a distinction between the size, intent and damage that lie behind lies. From fibs to whoppers, scams to hoaxes, fabrications to libel, we will look at the range of lying in this book.

Generally, lies can be categorised into two major groups – lies of omission where a speaker is being deceptive by leaving information out of what they are saying (this is why the law insists on 'the whole truth'), and lies of commission where a speaker is lying by presenting information as true when it is not. Throughout the book, we will consider how language is used for both categories of lies, along with a third type of lying: when speakers lie by telling the truth. We won't be considering why speakers lie or the psychology behind lying, but will focus solely on how lies can be revealed or indicated by the things people say and how they say them. I will use the terms 'lying' and 'deception' interchangeably throughout, for speakers who are imparting false information or concealing the truth.

As we concentrate purely on revealing lies in spoken language, we will leave aside discussions on non-verbal behaviour such as gestures and body language. Even though they have communicative relevance alongside language, as apparent indicators of deception these non-verbal cues may already be familiar to many of us and there is an abundance of deception detection literature on them. This is despite non-verbal cues not being that helpful in identifying lies[6] and the fact that some of these cues are actually false. For example, it is generally accepted, even across cultures,[7] that liars won't look you in the eye, but we know from scientific research that liars are very good at doing just that.[8] Similarly, assessments of the right or left/up or down direction of someone's eyes when they are speaking is also a fallacy in detecting lies.[9]

When speakers lie, their internal thoughts and emotions are displayed in their language.[10] The act of lying puts the speaker under mental stress; they must suppress the truth, invent the lie and also monitor how the lie is being assessed by whoever they are speaking to, while also monitoring their own behaviour and

## INTRODUCTION

remembering what they have said. This increases something called the cognitive load – the amount of mental resources used in working memory (our cognitive system that temporarily stores information). Liars may also experience heightened emotional arousal – fear of being detected, or satisfaction with not being detected. The increases in cognitive load and emotion reveal themselves in a speaker's language and make the cues to their deceit more discernible.

We will also only focus on lying and deception in spoken language rather than written (letters, emails, texts etc.), as written language can be constructed, edited and revised. Moreover, spoken lies tend to use different language than written lies. This is not only due to the interactive and contextual setting of spoken lies, but also because the communicative channel is oral and aural (mouth and ears) rather than visual and motor (eyes and hands), as with written language. We are all familiar with, or have experience of, sending an email or text communication that is misinterpreted by the receiver. This is primarily because some features of language termed 'paraverbal' or 'non-lexical' are not encoded in our written communication. Paraverbal information encodes our tone, pitch and voice quality (along with other signals), and this information carries how something is said, rather than what is said. We all know, for example, that a tone of voice can radically alter the meaning of what someone says, and so without this information, so much of what we write, especially in new media channels, can be misconstrued. Hence the rise of emojis.

Another way that spoken and written language use is different is that the use of lexical (nouns, verbs, adjectives) and grammatical (tense, pronouns, prepositions) words varies between these forms of communication. For example, when we speak we present something that happened as a process using verbs, whereas when we write, we present what happened as products by the use of something called nominalisation.[11] This is where verbs or adjectives are converted to nouns, so we are more likely to say: 'I admire him,' but more likely to write: '*He has my admiration.*' Written language in the form of statements and reports has a more formal style than spoken, and with the common use of word-processing programmes and now with AI, written language can be constructed, corrected, revised and edited before it is read by the receiver. As spoken language is immediate and spontaneous, self-corrections are heard by the listener and can be noted. In an email exchange, both communicators have time in which to prepare their responses, making language use more planned and considered, whereas this planning has a shorter duration in more instantaneous direct face-to-face communication – spoken in real time.

These examples show how language use differs between spoken and written communication. There are also differences of deceptive language use found in

## INTRODUCTION

speech and writing that should be analysed separately, otherwise they will give contradictory indications. For instance, recent research has started to look at how deceptive content can be recognised when people communicate by text messages. This research reveals that women will use longer messages when they are being deceptive, although there is no difference in the length of true or deceptive messages sent by men. This study also found that there was a higher use of first-person pronouns than second-person ones in deceptive text messages.[12] However, in particular cases a lower use of first-person pronouns is one of the major indications of deceptive *spoken* language. We will therefore concentrate on the things that people say and how they say them.

We will start our linguistic lie detection in Chapter 1 by looking at the words speakers use when they lie, or the words they should be using if they were telling the truth. We then move to Chapter 2, where certain grammatical and structural indications of lying can be revealed.

Chapter 3 focuses on the many forms of paraverbal information – the *way* we talk, such as voice pitch, voice quality and pauses, that can all be used to help detect whether a speaker is lying. And let's not forget that in spoken language, lies are usually told to someone in some form of social setting (at work, at home, during an interview or meeting). This means that in any analysis of language use we also need to consider the setting in which a lie is being told, and how language can be adapted, adjusted or changed depending upon where we are and who we are talking to. The importance of your role as the listener or conversational partner in detecting deception is discussed in Chapter 4.

My wish is that as a result of my sharing all this knowledge with you, you may be able to protect yourself and others from the damage that lies can do. Perhaps you already suspect you are being lied to? Perhaps you have suffered from someone's lies? Hopefully not as extreme as the personal case I told you about earlier, but you may have a partner who is difficult to trust, a colleague at work who fibs, a teenager who fabricates, a business partner who deceives, an employee/client/customer/patient who pretends, or a tenant or landlord who lies. I think many of us have. Maybe you have suffered from a stranger's lies, the careless driver, the bad tradesperson, the misleading seller/buyer, the devious professional, the fake Tinder date, the less-than-honest Airbnb guest/host. Perhaps you need to detect deception as part of your work; you might be a teacher, a government official, a police officer, a doctor or nurse, an insurance investigator, a lawyer, or of course a judge; you may work in recruitment, education, the media, or any other area where assessing the truth of what you are told is crucial. Maybe your livelihood or reputation could be damaged or ruined by liars; you are vulnerable to lies if you provide a service to strangers – restaurant owners, pub landlords,

## INTRODUCTION

hoteliers and holiday companies all encounter those fake reviewers, those fabricated stomach bugs. Lies affect all of us, in many ways.

Linguistic lie detection is a new and exciting field of research. We now know so much more about the indications of deceit and lies that have been hiding in a speaker's language all this time. The verbal indications presented to you in this book will help you understand more about the nature of how spoken language can give a liar away when they are lying or deceiving so that you can uncover the liar in your own life.

Oh, and if you're reading this because you want to learn how to hide your lies – bad luck! It's actually quite impossible.

CHAPTER 1

# Words: How to detect lexical lies

Let's start our exploration into linguistic lie detection with that most obvious element of any language – words. Commonly, words are considered to be basic units of language that carry meaning, so everything you are reading right now can be considered a word. However, to a linguist it's a bit more complicated and there is an ongoing debate on the definition of what a word is. Mainly this is because across languages, words come in all different shapes and sizes. Even though my field of linguistics finds the concept of what a word is a bit tricky to define, we will keep things simple and look at those words in this chapter which can be categorised as nouns, verbs, adjectives and adverbs. These are the big content or lexical words rather than smaller grammatical words which we will look at in the next chapter.

## Not naming names

People generally think that linguists analyse everything that others say – friends, family, colleagues, and anyone else that we come into contact with on a day-to-day basis. The truth is we don't. We would never have a conversation with anyone if we were constantly analysing their language. But there are many times when someone says something, which immediately switches us into language analysis mode.

One time, I was at home with the television on but not paying much attention, when a news story came on about a missing young girl. The girl's parents were being interviewed about the circumstances surrounding their daughter's disappearance. The father answered the journalist's questions, while the mother sat silent. At one point, the father said something that immediately caught my attention: it indicated that there was something highly suspicious in his claims about his missing daughter.

What was it that he had said that indicated he was lying about her disappearance? It was in how he named her.

Our names are extremely important. We are very protective of them, and we can easily be offended when other people forget, mispronounce or confuse them. We don't like names that remind us of people we dislike,

## HOW TO DETECT LEXICAL LIES

and we may not like it when people call their children or pets the same name as our own. Our names are usually decided by our parents, and depending on their choice you might end up being remembered either by being ridiculed or by attaining prestige. Names are powerful and most of us have more than those written on our birth certificates: pet names, nicknames, screen names, handles, stage names, pseudonyms, and names of affection or endearment. You are also named through your relationships with others: you might be a daughter, son, mother, father, friend, wife, husband, and so on.

We are also bestowed names (not all good) by other people. I have a friend called 'Big-Nose', and yes, he has a big nose, but he doesn't mind being called this as it's the name that those closest to him use. And this is what's so important about names: they can reveal other people's feelings towards us. They reveal our closeness with others, or the distance we want to keep between us.

You know how when you are angry with someone – like your partner or child – you might call them by their full name? When you lengthen their name, it reveals your emotional state towards them and how close you feel in your relationship in that moment. This is the magic of names. Because the names we use for other people can reveal our feelings; they can also reveal if we are lying. When we know and use a person's name, it means that there is a level of closeness or proximity. For example, we refer to our friends and family using first names or nicknames but use surnames when we refer or speak to teachers, bosses or anyone else that we don't know very well or don't have a familiar relationship with. Think of it like pulling people near to you when you use their first names and pushing them away when you don't.

Now, think about a time when you really disliked someone. Perhaps you disliked them so much that you could not even bring yourself to say their name and instead referred to them as 'that man' or 'that woman'. If you have ever owned a dog or cat and have returned home to find your pet has ruined your furniture, you will say 'that dog/cat', because you are upset with them. This is a natural response to distance yourself from the other person or creature as much as possible. We all use this push and pull of names multiple times a day without thinking about it.

This is what linguists refer to as distancing language. The different words we use to refer to others indicate immediacy or distance. This is why salespeople always ask to use your first name – it creates a closer connection and you become a bit more compliant. Here's some quick advice: never let someone who is trying to sell you something use your first name, and you'll be less likely to be manipulated into a sale.

Names as an indicator of our feelings towards others also really help in revealing when someone might be lying. Liars will try to get away or distance themselves from the person they are lying about. If a speaker refers to someone they know well, but rather than using their name or kinship words (like mother, brother, son etc.), they are creating distance, this might indicate that they are lying, particularly if the speaker shouldn't have any negative feelings towards the person they are talking about.

In some cases, people who are not telling the whole truth will try to distance themselves by referring to themselves in the third person. This is a form of self-reference known as illeism. For some speakers, it is thought illeism displays a narcissistic tendency, and there are lots of politicians who use it ('Thanks, Obama'). Donald Trump is quite well-known for his use of illeism – 'Nobody would be tougher on Isis than Donald Trump,' said Donald Trump. You see how it works? Illeism also creates distance as a form of emotional self-regulation, removing the speaker from themselves particularly in stressful encounters or situations. When Woody Allen complained to *CBS News* that many actors were refusing to work with him, he said: 'All they're doing is they're persecuting a perfectly innocent person and they're enabling this lie.'[1] He names himself as a third person – it's a strange way to speak, and perhaps he unconsciously does so as a way to emotionally regulate himself.

Going back to the news item I was watching; the journalist asks the father if he had ever tried to force his daughter into marriage. His response was: 'No, because the daughter does not want to be married yet.' His linguistic choice was highly unusual and marked. What it showed was that he was creating a very large distance between self and his daughter, which is a strong indication that he was lying in some way. He does not use her name or define his relationship to her (my daughter); instead his language shows a marked separation between himself and her – reducing her to the child of non-specific individuals ('the daughter').

Eventually, her body was found in a river. After a large police investigation, including a confession from the girl's sister, the father and mother were both charged and convicted of killing their teenage daughter. It was an honour killing. The parents had tried to force their daughter into an arranged marriage, and when she refused, they felt she had brought shame upon the family and so murdered her.

If you pay close attention to the way that people refer to others, you'll be able to see if distancing language is being used. If a speaker is trying to separate themselves from another person, you should ask yourself – is it because they are lying in some way?

Let's try this out. Have a look at the following two transcripts from real emergency calls. Who do you think is lying?

> **Caller A:** 'My daughter's husband . . . um . . . my son-in-law . . . um got in a fight with my daughter. I intervened and I think he's in bad shape. We need help.'[2]

## HOW TO DETECT LEXICAL LIES

**Caller B:** 'My my er son's friend is staying with us. Er this morning I tried to wake both of them up but the girl didn't wake up.'[3]

Did you think it was Caller A or Caller B who is the liar? Or did you think it was neither? Or maybe both? If you thought it was both callers, then congratulations. You're right. The names that both callers use for the people they are asking for help for is revealing – they are distant names.

Sometimes in emergencies, people who are involved in the harm or death of a person will phone for help. And if they try to distance themselves from the person they are calling about by referring to them in distancing language, it could be a sign they are lying about what happened. Caller A is a father-in-law who rang 911 to ask for the emergency services after getting into a fight with, and killing, his son-in-law. But he initially uses distancing language when he does not name him as his son-in-law but 'my daughter's husband'.

Caller B is a mother whose son murdered his girlfriend. The mother knows this when she calls 999, and so names the dead girlfriend as 'the girl' rather than 'my son's girlfriend', as we would expect. This mother and her husband were later jailed after it emerged that they had lied to the police to help their son cover up the murder.[4]

When I've been researching how emergency callers refer to the individual they are calling about, I've come across many cases of missing children. A clear pattern of deceit emerges from callers who refer to the child by their age rather than their relationship to the caller. Let me show you what I mean. In real-life emergency calls, deceitful callers have said things like: 'The door was open, there was a package outside and the three-year-old was not in the house,'[5] or: 'I just woke up and my three-year-old is missing.'[6] These callers were eventually found to be concealing their involvement in the death of the child. Compare this with innocent callers, who name the child based on their relationship with the caller: 'Hi, my daughter's missing and she's only two.'[7] The truthteller gives the age of the child as information, rather than as a way to name the child.

If you hear a speaker using distancing names for someone they know well (including themselves), be careful as it may show that they are trying to create a level of separation between themselves and that person. Depending on the situation, maybe you should not believe all that they are saying.

Our names are important markers of our identity. We all have little choice over what we are called. However, it is very difficult for a liar to change the way they name or refer to other people when they are trying to hide the truth. The names we use for other people show our feelings towards them, and as we have seen, can even reveal whether we are telling the truth about them or not.

# HOW TO DETECT LEXICAL LIES

## There's little sense in lies

Have you ever had something happen to you that motivated you to completely change your life and follow your dreams? Where you abandon your job, leave your home and do the thing you always wanted to do? A young man called Steve did. Something happened to him that was so shocking, he decided to leave his boring desk job working for a bank in New York and move to Los Angeles to pursue his dream of being a comedy entertainer. Life was too precious and it could all be over in an instant.

So Steve moved to California and, after just a few years of living in LA, his life was great. He managed to secure his first TV role on a top-rated show and went on to appear in films and TV comedies: his profile was steadily rising. He was becoming a star – the entertainer he had always wanted to be. He was becoming so well-known he was even given his own stand-up special show on Comedy Central TV. Leaving his old life behind to follow his dreams was the best decision he could ever have made. He was now a famous comedian and entertainer, enjoying the luxury lifestyle that went with his celebrity status. He had pursued his passion and it had all worked out wonderfully. His story was an incentive for others to follow their dreams.

But what was the event that led Steve to throw his life in the air, giving up his previous career and home?

It was 9/11.

On that fateful day, Steve had been working in the offices of Merrill Lynch on the fifty-fourth floor of the south tower of the World Trade Center.

'I was there and then the first tower got hit and we were like, jostled all over the place,' Steve told an interviewer in 2009. 'I still have dreams of like, you know, those falling dreams.' Just minutes before the next plane hit the south tower, Steve fled to the street. He recalled the moment, explaining: 'I couldn't tell exactly where it went in. So, I call up to the office, and it was pandemonium.'

He was lucky to be alive. It was this momentous, horrifying event that confirmed Steve's desire to change his life. Over the years since 9/11, Steve gave numerous interviews of his experience that day.

Each of them was a lie.

Steve had not been working in the twin towers. He was never there. He had made the whole thing up. What a comedian, indeed.

It was not until 2015 that the truth came out, when the *New York Times* investigated his claims and found he had been working in New York's Midtown district, nowhere near the twin towers. In analysing Steve's language from this interview, we can hear telltale signs that he was making it all up, long before any of his facts needed checking. And it has all to do with his lack of sensory-perceptual words in the descriptions of that terrible day.

Our memories of events are informed through our perception; what we saw, heard, smelt, felt and tasted, along with contextual information such as when something happened and where. When we recall events, we use words that describe the main five senses: auditive (hearing), visual (seeing), tactile (touching), gustative (tasting) and olfactive (smelling). Words such as rough, smooth, wet, damp, silent, noisy, loud, perfumed, dizzy, slump, hot, cold, bitter, windy, glance, snap, delicious, and so on, all describe sensory-perceptual experiences. We can also include words which describe our inner physiological condition (interoception) and our sense of balance, body position and movement (proprioception). These are some simple examples:

**Visual:** 'I glanced over my shoulder and saw he had a gun.'

**Auditive:** 'The bar was so noisy, we had to shout.'

**Gustative:** 'I knew my mouth was bleeding as I could taste metal.'

**Tactile:** 'His hands were cold and rough.'

**Olfactive:** 'His breath smelt of cigarettes and beer.'

**Interoception:** 'My heart was beating so loudly.'

**Proprioception:** 'I was hunched over; it made me feel dizzy.'

The language of liars usually lacks words which describe sensory-perceptual experiences.[8] Liars try to make up or imagine an event, so their constructed memories will contain more information about thinking processes and less about the sensory-perceptual details.[9] Though sometimes liars build on past experiences or knowledge, even these types of lies lack the richness of sensory words that are found in truth-tellers' accounts. What we should be on the lookout for is the absence of any real descriptive sensory details to signal if a story is fabricated.

In Steve's false account, he provides real no sensory-perceptual details of 9/11. He hears no screams, loud bangs or smashing glass, he doesn't smell burning or see fire and smoke. He only uses one descriptive word and that is 'jostled'. Steve might be jostled in a crowd but this adjective appears highly unusual in an account which describes being in a building that a plane has hit. There are no real descriptive details of this horrifying experience because Steve was not there, and it is difficult for him to build these descriptive details into his story. Based on that, we can and should be suspicious of what he says.

People who experience a major event will remember their experiences through their senses and refer to them when describing it later. Their recollections will be less about what they were thinking and more about how they experienced the event; what they saw, felt, heard, smelt and tasted. We should expect to find sensory language in stories from people who recall something shocking.

## HOW TO DETECT LEXICAL LIES

Like what happened to the top-rated NBC news anchor Brian Williams while covering the invasion of Iraq. A high-profile journalist, Williams was the longest-serving news anchor for the *NBC Nightly News*. His reporting coverage of Hurricane Katrina led to many awards and accolades, and in 2007, *Time* magazine named him as one of the 100 most influential people in the world. In 2003, even though Williams was not an experienced war correspondent, he was such a highly regarded journalist that he was given the assignment of being sent to Iraq to cover the US military's invasion. A dangerous job by any standards. Ten years later, in an interview with David Letterman, Williams recounted a terrifying experience he had when covering the Iraq War: 'Two of our four helicopters were hit by ground fire, including the one I was in.'

Shocked by Williams's experience, Letterman asks him what happened the moment he realised the helicopter had been hit. Williams replies: 'Erm, we figure out how to land – safely, and we did. We landed very quickly and hard and we put down and we were stuck.'

Did you notice there were no sensory-perceptual words? Why are these words missing from Williams's description? As an experienced journalist, Williams's job was all about words: writing, reporting, discussing and interviewing. Isn't it strange how he could be so dull in his account of being in a helicopter that was shot down?

Like Steve's story, his too was a lie.

Disasters, explosions, shootings, fires, wars or any other major catastrophic events create a sensory overload for witnesses. Heat, smells, sounds, burning, flashes, shrapnel, gunshots, screaming: all our senses take this information in, and it usually stays with us even with lesser critical events like minor car crashes. When people recall these events truthfully, we find that they use words or language which relate to their sensory-perceptual experience. They will describe the smashing glass, the screeching tyres, the burning smoke, the flash of light.

Take, for instance, this example. It was a Latin-themed event at the Pulse nightclub in Orlando, June 2016. One of Orlando's biggest nightclubs, Pulse was a popular spot for the LGBTQ+ community. The black-painted exterior of the large single-storeyed building, with its distinctive capital P road sign, was a familiar landmark on South Orange Avenue. It was a place where anyone could come and have a good time. Welcoming and inclusive to all, Pulse was always packed with crowds of people from all walks of life. That warm June night had been a real success, attracting over 300 clubbers enjoying the music and dancing.

Suddenly, the sound of rapid gunfire blasted throughout the nightclub. A gunman had opened fire on the terrified crowds with an assault rifle, killing at least forty-nine people and injuring many more. It was one of the worst mass shootings in recent US history.

## HOW TO DETECT LEXICAL LIES

Someone who said he witnessed the shootings told reporters the following:

> '. . . No it was like rapid fire like brrrrrrrr and then he'd like change put another ammunition brrrrrrrr and then change put another ammunition and I could just smell the ammo in the air and I was like this is a gun this is not a firework . . .'[10]

He recalls how he could 'smell the ammo in the air' and how this smell was from a gun and not from a firework. This is a truth-telling witness as he even mimics the gun firing to enhance the sensory-perceptual detail of how the 'rapid fire' sounded. His use of this type of language is what we would expect of someone who genuinely experienced the event they are recounting.

Whereas a liar will fill their fabricated accounts with what they were thinking, as thinking takes over from sensory perception when liars construct a story. Take, for example, Williams's response: 'Erm, we figure out how to land' – which is a cognitive or thinking description – when asked what happened the moment they realised their helicopter had been shot. He didn't reply that they realised they had been hit because there was an explosion, or a loud bang, shouting, or that they were holding on for dear life while the helicopter was rapidly losing height and speeding towards the ground. There's an imagined thought process instead.

Our comedian friend Steve is the same. While watching the second plane hit the south tower, he recalls: 'I couldn't tell exactly where it went in.' There's the cognitive process again (along with the lack of sensory-perceptual details). A passenger jet is flown into a skyscraper and all Steve can tell us of witnessing that moment is that he couldn't tell where the plane went in?

Watch out for those crash, bangs and wallops. If these sensory-perceptual words are not there in a person's story – you should ask yourself: are they really telling the truth?

## The truth is a bit more abstract

There is more to understand about how sensory-perceptual words are used and how these can be compared to other descriptive words when assessing the language of liars and truth-tellers. This is through understanding that lexical words (verbs, nouns and adjectives) can all be categorised on a scale from concrete to abstract.[11]

The most concrete words are known as Descriptive Action Verbs, such as jump, punch, run, slap, and so on, as these are typically directly observable. We can see Will slap Chris, or Will jump on to a step. Next on the scale are Interpretative Action Verbs, like pretend, help and hurt, which require some interpretation and knowledge of context. The context in the example 'Will hurt Chris' could be that Chris was hurt because Will slapped him. More abstract still are State Action Verbs, which refer to a single behavioural event – as in amaze, bore, surprise and upset. These usually require more clarification, such as, why was Chris upset? (Because Will slapped him.) State Verbs refer to enduring mental or emotional states which have no clear beginning and end, such as prefer, hate, admire, like and detest. 'Will hates Chris' is an enduring emotional state; we don't know when these feelings started. Finally, the most abstract category is Adjectives, like helpful, honest, reliable, nice and aggressive. Adjectives do not refer to any situation, so we have to interpret them from context, as they are detached from specific behaviours.[12]

Categorising words in this way can help us in determining 'psychological distance' (which we will look at more closely later on). We describe the positive behaviours of those whom we are close to using abstract words (she's wonderful), but we use more concrete words when we are not so close to the person we're talking about (she's good-looking). Yet we can see the opposite happen when we describe negative behaviour; we describe those we are close to with concrete words (he's tired) and those we are distant from with abstract ones (he's stupid).[13]

Abstract and concrete words are also used strategically by lawyers in court. In describing a defendant's actions (negative behaviour), prosecution lawyers typically use abstract language that ties a defendant's actions to their internal characteristics and personal responsibility (aggressive, angry, spiteful). However, defence lawyers will typically use more concrete language that focuses on the situation as the cause for the defendant's actions and therefore deflects the blame away from the defendant.[14] If we are on a crowded bus and it suddenly stops, leading another passenger to step on our foot, we are likely to ascribe this to their clumsiness (personal characteristic), whereas it was the situation (the bus stopping suddenly) which caused them to step on our foot. We all use this type of abstract and concrete language in our daily lives, but being attuned to how it is used can be a useful tool in guiding us to see if someone is telling the truth.[15]

Abstract language is found significantly more in truth-tellers' accounts. Concrete words are easier to ground in perceptual experience – for example, 'house' is a concrete word as it is grounded in experience and is easily recalled – whereas abstract words are harder to recall and not immediately grounded in perceptual experience. Liars are more likely to use a higher level of concrete words because they are easier to mentally retrieve than abstract ones, and as lying places greater cognitive load on a speaker, someone who is expending lots of mental energy making up a story will naturally gravitate towards words that are easier to retrieve from memory (concrete words). We would expect that a narrative account that encodes abstract language such as:

'I was upset at the hospital,' is more believable than an account with concrete language: 'I visited the hospital.' Abstract experience is a lot harder to invent.

When the Duke and Duchess of Sussex were allegedly chased through Manhattan by paparazzi, a member of their security team said: 'I have never seen, experienced anything like this. What we were dealing with was very chaotic. There were about a dozen vehicles: cars, scooters and bicycles. The public were in jeopardy at several points. It could have been fatal. They were jumping kerbs and red lights. At one point they blocked the limousine and started taking pictures until we were able to get out.'

If we look at the level of language abstraction when he speaks about this situation, we can see that his language contains mostly concrete words (seen, jumping, blocked, taking pictures). This appears quite strange, especially when he states that he had never seen or experienced anything like that before – we would expect to get more language describing the abstract experience of being in that situation. For example, we might expect: 'I felt quite scared and worried. There were so many vehicles, it was dark. I didn't know what would happen. I was trying to keep everyone safe, but we kept being surrounded by photographers. To my relief, we managed to get away.' Truthful accounts are more likely to include abstract words (scared, worried, happen, safe and relief).

Listening to individuals recounting their experiences is something that many people have to do for their job, like police officers, lawyers, journalists and doctors. With doctors or medics, their patients will usually describe how some injury happened. A typical case they might experience is the patient who has slipped/fallen/tripped and ended up with an object lodged in their rectum. Regardless of the implausibility of how the object came to be stuck in that particular spot, patients will invent lie after lie to save face in the hope the medics will believe that they are just the victim of an unfortunate accident. One patient trying to save face recounted their mishap as follows: 'I went to the bathroom about two thirty, three o'clock this morning. I've just moved into the property, so I haven't got carpets throughout. My bathroom floor was a bit wet, I slid off the toilet seat, right next to the toilet seat was a toilet brush and I've landed literally on it.'[16] The medics (and we) know he's lying, and his language use reflects his untruthfulness: there is nothing descriptive about the pain he must have felt, and his account is full of concrete words (slid, wet, landed).

It is not just medics that hear quite a few invented stories, we all have. It's quite common that people make up experiences that they never had, or that they've visited places they've never been to or done things that they haven't. Usually these might be innocuous tales told to impress others, to garner sympathy or to feel a sense of belonging. These types of lies should not concern us too much as there's little harm in them. However, other types of storytelling do create harm, like the comedian

## HOW TO DETECT LEXICAL LIES

Steve and his twin towers story. When these people lie by pretending they are survivors of some disaster or major trauma, it minimises the horrific or negative experiences of many others who have suffered these disturbing episodes, events or tragedies. But if we remember that when we hear someone recounting an experience and it has an absence of sensory-perceptual words and includes mostly concrete words, then we should be on alert as their account is most likely to be a story rather than a memory.

Let's test this out – see if you can detect whether our next narrator is telling the truth or not.

Growing up in the small central Polish town of Piotrków Trybunalski, Herman was only ten years old when the Nazi invasion of Poland took place in 1939. Herman, his family and thousands of others were rounded up and confined to one of the first Jewish ghettos. After enduring two years in this ghetto, Herman was tragically separated from his mother who was put on a train and sent to Treblinka. He would never see her again. Herman, along with his three older brothers, was sent to a sub-camp of the Buchenwald concentration camp.

He would survive this horrific experience and, after the camp was finally liberated by Allied troops, became one of hundreds of orphans who were brought to England at the end of the war. Years later he moved to New York, and in 1957, one of Herman's friends asked if he wanted to go on a blind date with a young woman called Roma. She too was a Polish Jew who had survived the Nazi concentration camps. Herman agreed, not knowing how this chance encounter with this young woman would change his life. The evening of his date arrived, but when Herman spoke with Roma, he realised he had met her many years ago while he was interned in the concentration camp. Every day, she had thrown apples to him over the barbed wire. He never knew the name of the girl who saved his life, until now. He asked her to marry him on the spot. She agreed. For years they lived happily as a married couple in New York and had two children together.

But who was Roma? Why did Herman think she had saved him? He recalled the story:

> 'A little girl was hiding behind a tree like that and she was looking up, alright? Looking over, and then I happened to see her and she stepped forward and I said to her "Do you happen to have something to eat?" in German so she would understand me and said it in Polish. And she took, she was wearing a nice warm coat, it was the middle of the winter, she was wearing a nice warm coat and she took out an apple from the tree from her pocket and stepped forward and threw it over the fence. I grabbed it and I started to run back. And that happened every day.'[17]

Is Herman recounting a memory or telling a fabricated story? Did he use abstract words or mostly concrete ones?

## HOW TO DETECT LEXICAL LIES

Over the years, he repeatedly told the story to friends and family: how his blind date Roma was the little nine-year-old girl that had thrown apples to him while he was in a concentration camp. In 1995, Herman decided to write up the story for a local newspaper's Valentine's Day competition. His story won and was featured on the front page of the *New York Post*. Soon after, a media frenzy descended upon the couple. Everyone wanted to hear more about this great love story – Herman and Roma even appeared on the *Oprah Winfrey Show*; she declared it as 'the single greatest love story'. Book deals in the millions were being signed for *Angel at the Fence*, a film adaptation was being put in place, interviews, television appearances, the demand for Herman and Roma to speak about their Holocaust love story was overwhelming.

Did you detect that Herman had indeed made it all up? There were no apples. Roma never came near to the concentration camp. They had never met before their blind date. The book was cancelled, so was the film adaptation, and the interview demands turned into ones questioning why Herman had lied. Most people thought it was simply for the money.

When Herman tried to justify his fabricated story, he said: 'In my mind, I believed it. Even now, I believe it.'[18]

Everyone believed it until some serious fact-checking went on, but if Herman's account of Roma throwing the apples to him is looked at closely, as you saw his description has no abstract or sensory language. There is nothing to suggest how Herman felt – would he not have been petrified in approaching the fence when anyone that did so was shot dead? In such a highly charged emotional setting, Herman's tale of receiving the apple from this young girl should be full of sensory words, yet there is nothing to suggest any valid experiential account in his language; instead it is full of concrete language.

What about this next story? True or false?

On 26 December 2004 one of the world's most devastating natural disasters in recorded history happened: an earthquake in the Indian Ocean triggered a series of tsunamis, resulting in the death of over a quarter of a million people. Ten years later, a survivor of this horrific event recounted her experiences of that terrible day:

> 'One moment that stays with me is when the wave crashed through the floors below. Hearing the glass shatter and people screaming, and at that point realising: 'This is really bad, my life is in danger.' Seeing people climbing trees and seeing people swept away. Hearing people screaming in different languages and not understanding. You heard that scream that people only have when their life is in danger. We were trapped on the second floor, looking on, for about eight hours. I was feeling absolutely terrified and the waves were getting bigger. We knew if that water reached us we didn't really stand a chance. We were so lucky that the hotel we were in was a

big modern building with strong foundations. I was really anxious that the foundations would go at some point because we were just being pummelled over and over by the water.'[19]

As you can see now, this account is from a truth-teller's memory: it is full of sensory-perceptual words (anxious, absolutely terrified, screaming, trapped, big, modern, strong, pummelled, shatter, crashed). Not only does she detail what she saw, but also what she heard and felt. She brings the experience alive in her description. We are invited to feel what she must have felt. Even though many years have passed, her language is full of details recording her senses, perceptions and experience. When we contrast this type of language use with those speakers who are not telling the truth, such as Herman, we see how language can reveal whether a story is being remembered or fabricated.

Descriptions which are empty of abstract or sensory-perceptual details should make us pay attention and consider whether the speaker probably wasn't where they said they were, or experienced what they said they did. Deceivers are more likely to use concrete language like plain motion words (move, go, walk) instead. Sensory descriptive words are colourful language and a good indicator of truth-telling.

And the most 'colourful' language of all is, of course, swearing.

## The truth about profanities

What constitutes profane language is different in each and every culture, but it usually includes obscene or taboo words,[20] swearing, sexual terms, racist or sexist insults/slurs, or any other offensive, blasphemous or vulgar words or phrases. Profanities are used as expressives: words that relate to the expression of emotions. For example, if we use a profanity like damn, as in 'damn car', it only differs from a phrase or sentence without its occurrence by indicating the emotional expression of the speaker's internal feelings about the car.

A range of emotions can be expressed using profanities, such as frustration, anger, hostility, pain[21] or surprise.[22] Our overall perception of people who use profane language is commonly unfavourable. We generally interpret its use as antisocial, aggressive or abusive. Our perception can also vary depending on context. We may not consider profanities in a film as that bad, but if those same profanities are spoken outside a primary school, our perception would (or should) be completely different.

Profanities violate our accepted social norms of language – we are brought up knowing that using swear words is socially unacceptable, and in certain countries their use in public is considered an offence. In England and Wales, if you use words which are threatening, abusive or insulting, or that cause or are intended to cause harassment, alarm or distress, you are committing an offence under the Public Order Act (1986) and can be prosecuted.[23] English law confirms that the use of profanities is a transgressive act – they violate social and moral boundaries. In the US, the first amendment can override any state laws on the use of offensive language, and if you live in Australia, you can receive a hefty fine for swearing in public.

Even though swearing may result in violating certain laws or social norms, did you know that it can show you are a more honest person?

Swearing or the use of profanities has long had an association with moral degeneracy and low education.[24] The belief still endures that people who swear are untrustworthy[25] and possibly have a deficit in other areas of their moral behaviour, such as that they lack generosity, honesty, integrity or kindness. But this is all it is – a belief. The actual truth that is emerging from research is that swearing indicates honesty.

As studies into swear words and swearing had been largely absent in the scientific literature, two social science researchers, Eric Rassin and Simone Van Der Heijden, decided to investigate whether the inclusion of swear words in testimonies increased the believability of those statements. Firstly, a group of seventy-six respondents were told that certain researchers propose that truthful statements can be distinguished from deceitful ones from their content. Then the respondents were asked to look at a statement that contained swear words and to choose between three options: were the profanities a sign of truthfulness, of deceit, or a non-discriminative characteristic?

Most respondents didn't believe that the inclusion of swear words discriminated between deceitful and truthful statements (46 per cent), but while 38 per cent believed that swear words were characteristic of deceitful statements, only 16 per cent believed that these words were indicative of credible statements. These results tally with the common assumption that the use of swear words corresponds more with deceit and dishonesty than with truthfulness and honesty.

However, this same study found that when the respondents were confronted with two versions of a statement from a fictitious suspect denying their involvement in a burglary, one which included swear words and one without, the one with swear words (damn, shitty, fucking) was considered more credible than the one that omitted them. The respondents were shown a statement containing a fragment of a verbatim description of an interrogation of a suspect. They were asked to read it carefully. This is what it said:

**Interrogator:** 'I ask you once again . . . were you involved in the burglary in the Havenstreet last month?'

**Suspect:** 'No, God damn it. As I have stated ten times, I have nothing to do with that. What is this all about? I have been here in this shitty room for almost two hours now. I want to go home, or I want to be allowed to talk to my attorney. What a fucking mess.'

The researchers tested this result with a third study whereby participants evaluated the credibility of a different statement that included swear words and one that removed them. The results were similar to the second study: the statements that contained swear words were perceived as more credible. What this study concludes is that, even though swearing is thought to indicate deceit, when we are exposed to this language in use it actually increases the believability of statements.[26]

Further research which has analysed natural spoken and written patterns of language use has also disputed the association between dishonesty and profanity, as it strongly finds that a higher rate of profanity use is associated with more honesty.[27] So those awful f-bombs are a good sign of truth-telling, especially perhaps when speakers are denying false allegations made about them.

In Perth, Australia, a female shopkeeper was found murdered. The police initiated a murder inquiry and drew up a list of potential suspects, mainly local junkies, petty thieves and other undesirables. A man called Andrew was brought to their attention. He seemed like the kind of guy that would have committed such a crime: a petty thief with mental health issues, who had no job and was a known user of marijuana. An eyewitness apparently saw someone matching Andrew's description and the police thought they had further proof that Andrew was in the area where the murder took place at about 5 p.m., as he had run off without paying his fare from a taxi that dropped him to a nearby street. Bingo! The police had their man.

Even though there was no forensic evidence linking thirty-one-year-old Andrew to the murder, the circumstantial evidence seemed overwhelming. Yet he denied it wholeheartedly. 'I didn't fucking kill Pamela Lawrence,' Andrew shouted when questioned. 'I didn't fucking kill Pamela Lawrence. I was not in the fucking shop. I wasn't in the fucking shop.'

The police told Andrew to settle down, but he retorted: 'I won't fucking settle down! I didn't fucking do it and I'm not a fucking murderer! I didn't kill Pamela Lawrence. This is a murder and I didn't do it. Fuck, fuck, fuck, I didn't do it.'[28]

Andrew was questioned for over twelve hours without a lawyer present, and was finally charged with Pamela's murder. He was convicted with the only piece of evidence being some unsigned handwritten notes by the interviewing officers who claimed Andrew had confessed to the murder. He was sentenced to thirty years' life imprisonment in a maximum security jail.

Never believing that Andrew had committed this

murder, his family fought for many years to have his case re-examined. In 2006, after he had spent almost twelve years in prison, the High Court of Australia quashed his conviction and Andrew was released. He hadn't murdered Pamela, and there was no real evidence.

In Andrew's interview with the police, he swore – a lot. His answers were full of expletives. Andrew was telling the truth when he said he didn't kill Pamela, and his expletive-ridden denial was a good indication that he was doing this. Just ask emergency call handlers, who every day will hear expletives, swearing or even abusive language when people are calling in moments of heightened stress and emergency.[29]

The reason why truth-tellers are more likely to swear is because it displays the unfiltered genuine emotions of anger and/or frustration, particularly in denials. Swearing is commonly related to the display of these emotions, including surprise,[30] especially when falsely accused of something quite serious just like Andrew was.[31]

## It wasn't me

Fake news is nothing new.

In the early 1990s, Denver TV reporter Wendy Bergen had found a hard-hitting story: illegal dog-fighting was rife in the city. Gamblers were secretly congregating in basements and old warehouses, betting on bloody, vicious and criminal dog-fights. Wendy's exposé 'Blood Sport' was a four-part series featuring horrific close-up shots of dogs ripping each other apart and interviews with disguised dog-fighters. The story was a disturbing revelation for Denver residents who had no idea that dog-fighting was 'big business'.

Wendy's 'Blood Sport' exposé was exactly the kind of shocking investigative journalism that her bosses at the TV station had come to expect of her. But they wouldn't realise just how shocking it would really be.

Violent footage of two pit bulls fighting had been sent anonymously on a home-made VHS tape to Wendy. The tape also included recorded interviews with disguised gamblers and quotes by sources with their identities hidden. Wendy now had the evidence to show the viewers that the secret world of illegal and horrific dog-fighting was prevalent, but she needed more videos, and a source instructed her to turn up at a disused area by the river to film one of these dog-fights directly.

Wendy and her cameraman recorded graphic footage showing two snarling pit bulls charging at each other and fighting savagely, until one dog bit down on the other's head. Horrifyingly, one of the dog-fighters prised the dog's jaws apart by ramming a screwdriver into its mouth. Loosening its grip, the dog howled in pain. The video was certainly disturbing, and it was so graphic that it needed editing down before it aired for fear of being too extreme.

## HOW TO DETECT LEXICAL LIES

When other journalists and editors at the station looked at Wendy's recordings, something was not quite right with the footage. If dog-fighting was so prevalent, then why was it always the same two dogs fighting on Wendy's recordings? If illegal gambling was rife, where were the gamblers and spectators supposedly watching these fights? There only seemed to be a couple of spectators in the videos.

As suspicion grew that there was something amiss about Wendy's footage, journalists from other news agencies started to examine it more closely. Finally, direct allegations were made by another broadcaster that the video had been staged. Wendy vehemently denied this. Regardless of her denials, the allegation triggered a police investigation, and it didn't take them long to find and identify the two dogs on the tape. They concluded that the tape was a hoax.

In other words, it was fake news.

Over the next few months, the set-up of this 'fake news' piece was uncovered. Wendy had been contacted by a source who claimed that illegal dog-fighting was rife in Denver. This source then organised the dog-fight for Wendy and her cameraman to record. When they arrived for the recording, neither of them was suspicious that they were the only ones in attendance. They didn't even question the absence of hordes of illegal gamblers and spectators. They filmed their piece and left.

It was this recording that Wendy would edit to make it

look like an amateur home-video and claim that she had received other videos sent anonymously. Her fake exposé didn't only ruin her illustrious career and reputation, it also meant that Wendy was facing time behind bars for illegal dog-fighting herself. In Colorado, even just attending a dog-fight is in violation of the law. Regardless of the fact that it had been staged, Wendy's attendance at this event meant that she was charged and convicted of dog-fighting, along with conspiracy to commit dog-fighting and being an accessory to dog-fighting. Wendy's lack of prior convictions helped to persuade the judge against imprisoning her, and she was ordered to pay a $20,000 fine and complete 100 hours of community service.

Reflecting later on her fake news story, Wendy said: 'The anonymous tape – that was deceptive and unethical.'[32]

Do you see what Wendy did when she said that? She removed herself from her role in the lie. It was the anonymous tape which was deceptive and unethical, and not the person who made it – Wendy. She didn't say: 'I was deceptive and unethical.' She hid from being the deceiver.

There are many people who try to hide their role or responsibility when they do something bad. One way that these people do this is by grammatically reducing 'agency' in what they say (we will look at this more later on in the book). This is why it is common for liars to say something like: 'It just happened.' Nothing 'just happens' – it happens because someone has made it happen – but by framing it in a passive form, liars reduce their personal responsibility or involvement. This is a form of deceptive denial and is a way to maintain self-esteem. This is because when we do something bad or wrong, there is a discrepancy between our view of ourselves (as a good person) and our behaviours (bad).[33]

Have a look at what this young woman said when she had to testify in court:

'The gun just went off. I only wanted to break free from his grasp.'

Does a gun just go off or does someone have to pull the trigger? This woman is being deceptive: she shot her boyfriend twice, once in the head and once in the shoulder.[34] When someone who is lying reduces their agency it shows us that they are aware that their behaviour is wrong and they are trying to hide it. People who are telling the truth or who 'own' their actions will usually not reduce their agency. We will look at this in more detail in Chapter 2.

## Repetition, repetition, repetition

My partner sometimes lets out a little woodland cabin in the grounds of his house in the countryside. It's a nice, secluded place to escape to for a few days, and he supplies things like bottled water, tea, coffee, cutlery, firewood and other essentials for guests. Usually, he greets the guests when they arrive and gives them a quick tour of the cabin and the grounds. One afternoon, he had to stay late at work when a couple in their early forties and their dog turned up so I volunteered to show them around instead. The first thing they said to me was: 'Hi, nice to meet you. It's our wedding anniversary.'

This triggered my forensic linguistic switch and so I listened closely to what they said. I replied politely, congratulating them on their anniversary, and started to show them around. As we walked, they kept telling me things about themselves – how they were Christians, they were good people, they cared for an autistic child and looked after a sick parent, and did lots of voluntary work. They were more concerned with repeating what good people they were than taking in where they would be staying. I finally managed to leave them to enjoy their stay and returned to my partner's house. When he arrived home, he asked me what the guests were like. I told him that I thought there was something deceptive about them and they had put me on alert. I explained that it was because they kept repeating what good people they were. They were desperate for me to form a good impression of them. Perhaps unsurprisingly, when my partner went to clean the cabin after they left the next day, he found that they had stolen most of the supplies, including cutlery, glasses, dog bowls, towels, the kettle, even the extra toilet rolls. Not such good people after all.

We should watch out for any form of repetition in

language as it can indicate a heightened level of deception in what a speaker is saying.[35]

In February 2015, sixteen-year-old Becky from Bristol went missing, without taking any clothes or money. Becky had not told anyone that she was leaving, but her phone and laptop were missing as well. Her disappearance was a total shock to her family. Concerned for Becky's well-being, the police made a public appeal for information on her whereabouts. Becky's stepbrother Nathan and his girlfriend Shauna told the police that they heard Becky leave the house on that day she disappeared, and offered to help with the inquiries.

During an interview, the police asked Shauna to recall her memory of Becky leaving.

> '. . . Um then we came back up went into the kitchen to get a drink I think and wash my hands then I heard the front door slam um carried on washing my hands went into the living room and then I think it wasn't until a lot later on that Angie asked me if Becky had gone out and I said yeah I heard the door go she must have gone out earlier washing my hands I think I heard the door slam . . .'[36]

Becky never left the house alive. It may be a strange coincidence that Shauna keeps repeating that she was washing her hands when she was later convicted of the manslaughter of Becky and assisting in dismembering

Becky's body before hiding it in a shed. We expect that washing her hands afterwards was a real experiential detail that she could not conceal, either through guilt or the burden of the memory. Another repetition in her account is that she heard the front door slam, but the last time she mentions it she changes it to: 'I think I heard the door slam . . .' Within a few sentences she equivocated on the surety of her knowledge.

Repetitions of phrases or words is a strategy that enables liars to appear to be helpful by providing what could be assumed as more information or details in their accounts, while in truth saying nothing new. Liars invent all or part of their accounts and, if these accounts are unplanned, they construct them in real time as their narration develops. They cannot activate new information from memory, so they end up repeating themselves or saying the same thing in a different way. Doing so is an excellent way to reduce opportunity for self-incrimination and fill conversational space.

Aside from those individuals who are hard of hearing, when a speaker answers a question with another question, or asks for a question to be repeated, it can signal that the speaker is having difficulty retrieving the requested information.[37] If someone is being deceptive, this technique can be a way of avoiding answering straight away in order to buy time to compose themselves, or to concoct an answer. Especially when the question may be unexpected, when the speaker is lying they will need to stall

## HOW TO DETECT LEXICAL LIES

for time by repeating it back or asking for the question to be repeated. This tactic allows more planning time for their response.

We can see this technique being used by Jerry Sandusky in a televised telephone interview. Sandusky, an infamous US football coach, was convicted of child sex abuse over a fifteen-year period. The interviewer asks him: 'Are you sexually attracted to young boys, to underage boys?' Sandusky replies by repeating the question: 'Am I sexually attracted to underage boys?'[38] He goes on to deny that he is sexually attracted to underage boys, but was later found guilty of sexual crimes against children.

A familiar saying is that if a lie is repeated often enough, it becomes the truth. This is a real phenomenon known as the Illusory Truth Effect, whereby statements that are repeated are perceived to be truthful, even if they contradict our knowledge. In fact, the Illusory Truth Effect functions better when statements are easier to comprehend and process.[39] We can see that politicians, marketeers and advertisers all use easy repetitive slogans in their campaigns or advertising – 'fake news', 'eat fresh', 'because you're worth it' – in the hope that the general public starts to believe it. The Illusory Truth Effect (sometimes known as the Repetition Truth Effect) is quite a robust phenomenon in psychological research. Various mental processes have been investigated to help us understand why repetition increases subjective truth (our perception that something is true). A combination of reasons for this have been proposed, such as that repetition is found to increase processing fluency. This is part of our cognitive bias whereby our opinion of something is influenced by how easy or difficult it is to process or understand it. Repetition facilitates our processing and understanding and subsequently increases our believability. Familiarity through repetition is another mental process that contributes to subjective truth, as psychological studies into this have found that repeated information *feels* more true. This also corresponds with frequency as the higher occurrence of something increases our perception of its validity.[40] The more people that say the same thing, the more likely we are to just accept it as true; for example, do you believe that we should never wake up a sleepwalker or that we only use 10 per cent of our brains? These 'facts' are repeated so often that we assume they are true. When in fact, they are not.

On a functional level, the association between repetition and truth is therefore quite a striking effect. Which also means that repeating something to ourselves can make it seem 'more true', and in lie detection it is important to consider how individuals actually start to believe the lies they keep repeating. Lance Armstrong, the professional US cyclist, was involved in the biggest doping scandal in cycling history. When he finally admitted that he had been lying for many years about not taking performance-enhancing drugs, he explained: '. . . I viewed this situation as one big lie that I repeated a lot of times.'[41]

We have to be careful when speakers start to believe their lies, as their language and communicative behaviour will shift so that it does start to appear more truthful. Indications of deceit reduce as the liar's self-belief increases, especially if they have multiple opportunities in which to repeat their lies.

What this means is that the initial telling of a lie offers the most important insight into deceptive language or behaviour. Without the opportunity to repeat their lie, the speaker will talk with the conscious self-knowledge that they are lying, and we can expect more of the telltale markers of deception.

## Specifically lies

In March 2018, while out with her family in a small English town, sixteen-year-old Abigail saw a grey-haired man in his sixties and a thirty-something-year-old woman collapsed on a public bench. Thinking that the man had suffered a heart attack, Abigail and her mother rushed over to administer first aid. Being a nurse, Abigail's mother was able to examine the collapsed couple, but they presented with quite sinister symptoms; there was vomit by the bench, the woman was foaming at the mouth, and her eyes were completely white. Both the man and the woman were in a catatonic state.

Other people would be forgiven for having walked past the couple thinking they were high on drugs, even though they didn't look like typical drug-takers. It was also a strange place to take drugs: sitting on a public bench outside a busy shopping centre in the middle of the afternoon. Abigail's mother, a passing doctor, and the police and medics who were called to assist had no reason to suspect there was something seriously wrong with this couple. While the couple were admitted to hospital in a critical condition and put into intensive care, the police and medics started to report unusual symptoms in themselves: itching eyes and difficulty breathing. The man and woman had symptoms of paralysis of the nervous system. Tests sent to the UK government's laboratory confirmed what the hospital suspected – the couple had been poisoned by a nerve agent and those who had come into contact with them had also been contaminated. Far from being local junkies, the man was in fact a Russian ex-KGB spy and the woman his daughter – and they were victims of a targeted assassination. The small English town of Salisbury would become the focus of an international spy hunt.

Quickly sealing off the area where the couple were found, counter-terrorism officers searched for where they had come into contact with the nerve agent. Perhaps the poison had been put in the couple's food when they dined at a local Italian restaurant just before being found, or maybe they had been targeted in the street. Everywhere was being searched, and the town went into a state of emergency. Meanwhile, a police officer who had been sent to search the Salisbury home of the ex-KGB spy was urgently admitted to hospital, also with nerve agent poisoning. The source was found: the nerve agent had been sprayed on to the handle of the man's front door. But who had sprayed it?

It didn't take long for the intelligence services to identify who was responsible. As an ex-KGB officer who was given refuge in England after defecting from Russia, the man was a clear target for assassination. The UK government accused Russia of attempted murder, and a diplomatic row ensued. Although Russia would vigorously deny the accusations, six months and an intensive investigation later, the UK government released the names and photos of two Russian nationals alleged to have carried out the attempted assassination. They were believed to be active members of Russian military intelligence. Details emerged that showed their movements from when they arrived in the UK, their visit to Salisbury and their speedy departure. As their faces and identity were spotlighted across the global media, these would-be assassins were interviewed on Russian television, protesting their innocence, although confirming that they had visited Salisbury during the time the couple were poisoned:

**Interviewer:** 'On the CCTV footage from London, you walk in those now famous coats and sneakers in Salisbury. Are these people you?'

# THE LANGUAGE OF LIES

**Both spies:** 'Yeah, that's us.'

**Interviewer:** 'What were you doing there?'

**Spy 1:** 'Our friends had been suggesting for a long time that we visit this wonderful town [Salisbury].'

**Spy 2:** 'There's this famous Salisbury Cathedral, famous not only in Europe but in the whole world. It's famous for its 123-metre spire, it's famous for its clock – one of the first ever created in the world still working.'[42]

Even though most people viewing this interview suspected that these spies were lying, they further call into question their veracity by being so specific in their claims of being tourists. When Spy 2 mentions the specific height of Salisbury Cathedral's spire, it should immediately raise suspicion. When a speaker is being unusually specific about irrelevant information in their narrative, it indicates that their lies might have been planned.

We assume that what a person says is more likely to be true if it includes lots of details, as a liar is less likely to include details that could implicate them in some way, and it involves having to remember more. This is specificity of information. Because we think that all liars will avoid imparting information, we might assume that as we are being offered lots of information, the information must be true. This is not so. It depends on the content of what a person says, rather than the amount. This is especially relevant when the liar has had the opportunity to plan what they will say, and more so when their conversational partner is suspicious; liars speak longer than truth-tellers.[43] When liars include lots of unnecessary detail it is because they are using the strategy of persuasiveness. They will elaborate in these instances to make their account appear more believable, just like our spies did. A liar's elaboration is expected in an interactive context where they are trying to decrease their conversational partner's suspicion.[44] This is a different strategy from when a liar is trying to conceal information as they will avoid elaborating and reduce what they say, which we look at a bit later on.

Including more details as a form of persuasive deception is also what we find in 'swatting' calls. Originating from the online gaming world, swatting is a recent type of hoax call to emergency services to get SWAT teams or armed police to respond to reports of a hostage or murder situation. The fake caller gives another gamer's address, sending these heavily armed police teams to raid them. Recently, these hoax calls have been targeting celebrities who are now victim to having their homes stormed by armed police. In the US, the seriousness of these fake calls is reflected in the charge of domestic terrorism for swatting someone. In the first swatting prosecution, a fifteen-year-old boy called the police so that SWAT teams would raid the homes of other gamers. In one of these calls, the boy falsely claimed there was a murder and hostage situation and when SWAT teams raided the other gamer's home, they shot and critically injured the gamer's father. The identity of the hoax caller was found out, and he is now serving twenty-five years to life in a federal prison.[45]

These hoax calls are more than harmless pranks: not only are they a distraction and waste of resources, they are also putting people's lives at risk by sending armed police units to innocent homes. A common detail is the inclusion of the type of gun used, an example of specific but unnecessary information being shared:

**Call 1:** 'Hi, er I just I just killed my dad. He wouldn't give me my Xanax. I have an AK-47 and I just shot him in the face because he wouldn't give me my Xanax.'[46]

**Call 2** [a dispatcher explains what the caller said]: 'It looks like our male caller says he shot his girlfriend in the head with a 9 millimetre. He also said he tied his young daughter up in the bathroom. He's debating if he wants to kill her.'[47]

**Call 3:** 'In the chest, my dad has a licensed AR-15 in the closet and I took it out and I shot her.'[48]

In fact, these callers don't give generic gun categories (shotgun, pistol, rifle) but will often specify the make and style of the gun. In the transcript of Call 3, this caller further embellishes his hoax by specifying that the gun is licensed, that it's his father's, and details where his father keeps it (in the closet) – as if that would make a difference.

When the language of hoax callers is contrasted with the available and legitimate online emergency recordings of people using guns, we can spot patterns emerging. Most notably, genuine callers do not state the exact type of gun used. For emergency operators or dispatchers, listening out for this detail may assist them with differentiating between real calls and those that are swatting innocent people, or at the very least get them to pay closer attention. If a speaker is saying something too specific and unnecessary (especially when it is irrelevant in their answer to a question or when they are trying to persuade someone like an emergency operator), then it increases the likelihood that they are fabricating what they are saying.

Around the time I was doing my PhD, I was at a dinner party with some of my friends and their partners. One friend was expecting her boyfriend to turn up after he had finished work. This was in the pre-smartphone days, so my friend had no way of seeing if her boyfriend had left work and her texts had gone unanswered. He didn't arrive for quite a long time, missed the dinner and turned up just as the party was finishing, apologising that he had been stuck at work and that his phone had run out of battery. He then went on to explain in minute detail the tasks that had kept him occupied. It was all pretty uninteresting. My friend didn't seem that bothered and accepted that he was late, brushing it off as the result of his demanding job. He kept apologising and had the appearance of being genuinely remorseful, but I felt there was something suspicious about how specific he was being about what had kept him at work. Thinking it wasn't my place to get involved, I kept my thoughts to myself and said nothing to my friend. A few months later, she found out he had been having an affair with a co-worker, and that evening had been the beginning of it. So those superfluous but specific details about his work were the likely indicators of his deception.

## Don't believe, believe

One word that you might want to be on the lookout for is the word 'believe'. To believe is to accept that something is true, particularly without proof, and is used as a guarded affirmation,[49] usually to infer uncertainty.

But it is also used strategically as a way of deceiving others.

## HOW TO DETECT LEXICAL LIES

In 1994, executives from seven major tobacco firms were questioned by US House of Representatives' congressmen on the health risks of tobacco products. When asked whether cigarette smoking causes cancer, the CEO of one of the firms replied: 'I don't believe that.'[50] And despite overwhelming evidence to the contrary, when asked under oath about tobacco being highly addictive, each of the seven CEOs replied with similar answers: 'I believe nicotine is not addictive' and: 'I don't believe that nicotine or our products are addictive.' The US Department of Justice intended to prosecute these CEOs for perjury (as the scientific evidence proves the link between tobacco, and cancer and addiction), although the prosecution had to be abandoned because of the challenge in prosecuting anyone for their belief. It is not inconceivable that the CEOs had rehearsed their answers, knowing that the word 'believe' would protect them from persecution for perjury.[51]

The word 'believe' pops up frequently in the domain of 'snake-oil' pedlars – those who prey on the vulnerable and desperate by selling proposed cures for every known illness. These cures, which range from the downright crazy to the more plausible sounding, are get-rich-quick schemes for those who peddle them. There is a very long, and ever-growing, list of alternative health providers who sell 'miracle' cures, promoting some alternative therapy approach without any rigorous scientific support. These pedlars will often state that they believe their product works. A man called Dr Robert O. Young marketed an alternative approach to improving health called the 'pH Miracle', which claimed that maintaining the right pH balance in the body leads to an improved immune system and can combat serious illnesses. Young's ideas were developed into a series of books which sold in the millions, with promises like: 'If you want to lose weight and prevent or reverse diseases like diabetes, you can follow the guidelines in the pH Miracle.' Young also set up a treatment centre outside San Diego, California, known as the pH Miracle Ranch, with one area being a clinic for treating cancer patients.

The US authorities, becoming aware of Young's activities, duly investigated him, leading to his prosecution for practising medicine without a licence. He was sentenced to jail for over three years in 2017, and in court it was found that not only did Young not have a licence, but he wasn't even a medical doctor: he'd bought his doctorate from a diploma mill.

A year after being convicted of practising medicine without a licence, Young was sued by an ex-client. Young's claims about curing cancer with the pH Miracle led to a judge ordering him to pay $105 million in damages to another woman whose cancer was not cured by his programme. After this ruling, Young's attorney said: 'No matter if you believe in the pH Miracle or disbelieve it, it's clear that Robert [Young] believes it. He sincerely believes what he is doing.'[52] There we are then. Young's belief in his miracle means that it must work, even though clear evidence, such as the loss of lives, shows it doesn't.

Essentially, when a speaker relies on their belief in something, it's a way of being economical with the truth while protecting themselves from being called a liar.

Recent research has found that belief is not just about being protected from being called a liar, but also has a very strong role to play in distorting an individual's perception of the truth. When individuals strongly believe in something, despite knowing it to be false, the more vividly they imagine it the more they think it is true; even when faced with compelling evidence to the contrary.[53] Be on your guard if you hear 'believe', as you're probably dealing with how someone wants the world to be rather than what is factually true. And perhaps now more than ever before we should heed the advice of the little-known nineteenth-century philosopher William K. Clifford, who stated that: 'It is wrong always, everywhere, and for anyone, to believe anything upon insufficient evidence.'[54]

Language is revelatory. The words we choose, whether we swear or not, our use of sensory-perceptual words, or concrete and abstract ones, and how specific we are in what we say, can all help differentiate the truth from lies. But the language of lies is not just in these big lexical words, but in all elements of speech, including those little grammatical words like pronouns, articles, tense and aspect. This is what we'll look at next to add to our armoury of lie detection.

CHAPTER 2

# Grammar: How to detect lies of little changes

Most people will see the word 'grammar' and lose interest. After all, as well as not being particularly exciting, isn't grammar simply a set of rules about what you can and can't say? This is called prescriptivism – telling people how to use language in a supposedly 'correct' way. But I'll let you in on a secret: linguists don't mind if what you say is grammatical or not. It don't bother us. We study language with a descriptivist approach – what that means is we describe how languages are rather than tell people how to use them. Grammar is less about a list of rules and more a way to describe how sentences are ordered or structured, and how words are as well. In this chapter, we'll be looking at different small parts of speech (the grammatical words) – such as pronouns and demonstratives – along with verb tense and aspect. We will also look at the different ways that sentences and stories are structured so you can assess the likelihood of whether what you are hearing is truthful or not.

## Distance and lies

One area of linguistic lie detection that's particularly revealing is the way that speakers use space and distance when referring to other people or things. Before we look at how this occurs in a liar's language, we need to understand the importance of space and distance. Think for a moment about why we instinctually avoid sitting near people we don't like. And why if we find something offensive, we try to get as far away from it as possible. We create physical distance from people or things that we have a negative reaction to. This is called a flight response and it helps us to avoid harm or threats. We physically separate ourselves from potential harm, and the greater our dislike or negative feeling towards the person or thing, the greater the distance or flight response we have. We create safety by creating space. It's a basic survival mechanism.

Space and distance, or spatial relationships, are found to be one of the earliest concepts acquired in human development.[1] This can also be seen in language acquisition, whereby children will use spatial words or phrases earlier than they use temporal ones. For example, a child will use the word 'in' to define a spatial relationship ('she is *in* the house') far more and far earlier than they use 'in' to define a temporal point ('I will do it *in* a bit'). Words which refer to points in space such as here and there are used by children before they use points in time words like now and then. Children will also ask questions relating to space earlier than those relating to time. A child will ask and respond to where something or someone is before asking or answering questions of when something happened. Our concept of space – where we are in the world and in relation to other objects and people – is one of our most basic psychological functions.

Deeply ingrained into our biological make-up is the principle of 'distance equals safety'.[2] But we create safety through space or distance not only by physically removing ourselves, but also through creating what is known as psychological distance. Psychological distance is a cognitive separation of ourselves from other things such as persons, events or times[3] – the sense we have of how far or close something or someone is from ourselves – and it can profoundly influence our behaviour.[4] For example, this is why 'time heals'. The further away in time we are from a distressing event reduces our emotional intensity of that event or our responses to it.

Variations in psychological distance can affect our thoughts and emotional perceptions. Research from psychology shows that when people are primed (introduced to one stimulus to see how they respond to a subsequent stimulus) with an unconscious feeling of a congested space (like being in a lift/elevator), it increases their emotional discomfort when reading an embarrassing text as opposed to those who were primed with a wide-open space.[5] Their responses to an extremely violent prompt has the same basic results – people who had been primed with a congested space found the violence more aversive than those who had been primed with an open space. These results can be explained by the brain's connection between distance and safety. If boundaries are closer (or there is a feeling of being hemmed in) then we have a greater emotional response to perceived threats. Just think of travelling on the underground or subway during rush hour: as space is hugely reduced, emotional responses are heightened.

Here's a trick: we can reduce emotional intensity if we increase the psychological distance. Distance can be created psychologically by recalling personal memories as if you were an observer or an outsider, rather than immersed in the memory – the actor. If you were to recall an instance when you felt overwhelming anger or hostility, but then imagine yourself stepping back and moving away and observing, you will notice your feelings of anger subside – whereas if you recall the instance as if it were happening again, your anger towards it is less likely to change.[6]

Whenever we recall autobiographical events from a first-person perspective it makes those events psychologically nearer.[7] In other words, imagine watching the child you were (third person) in a memory as opposed to inhabiting your child self again (first person). In fact, this technique is so effective that it is used in therapy to reduce the emotional experience people have when they recall a negative or damaging experience. This difference in perspective from first person to third person also affects how we attribute reason for our past behaviours. A third-person or observer's perspective means we are more likely to attribute our behaviour to personality traits rather than a first-person perspective, which attributes behaviour to specific situational factors.[8] For example, if you were to observe yourself (third-person perspective) from a moment in the past where you lost your temper with someone, you are more likely to attribute your behaviour (losing your temper) to being an impatient or easily frustrated person, whereas if this instance is viewed as if you are reliving it (first-person perspective), then you may attribute your behaviour to the other person's actions instead.

What's important for us to know when it comes to lying is that psychological distance is encoded in language. When something is physically close to us, we use 'this/these', and when that something is more distant, we refer to it as 'that/those'; for instance, 'this book' is closer to us than 'that book'. But we also make these distinctions when something or someone is emotionally near or far from us, or when we want to indicate our separation or closeness. Our choice of words, grammar and sentence structure reveals our attitudes and feelings.

We've already explored this when it comes to word choice in the previous chapter – the concept that when you are annoyed or angry with someone, you are less likely to call them by a name that reflects your intimacy. Similarly, you might refer to them by using 'that' rather than 'this' ('that man/woman/dog' rather than 'this man/woman/dog'). This is called the distal demonstrative, and it is an indication that we hold a negative stance towards someone or something, not necessarily that they are physically far. It shows that we are creating psychological distance between us and whatever it is that we don't want to be associated with.

When we hear people use this type of distance in language, we should ask ourselves why. Why is it they want to create psychological safety through using distanced language?

Most people only dream of winning the lottery, but for Abraham Shakespeare, this dream-come-true would turn into a nightmare. In 2006, the forty-one-year-old truck driver won the $30 million jackpot on the Florida lottery. After buying himself a house, a car and a second-hand Rolex watch, Abraham felt compelled to give his winnings away – mostly to those who simply asked him for it. But the constant demands from family, acquaintances, hangers-on and even strangers brought Abraham down. He complained to his childhood friend that: 'I thought all these people were my friends, but then I realised all they want is just money.' A year after winning the lottery, and with his fortune rapidly dwindling, Abraham befriended a woman who was writing a book on how people were taking advantage of him. Forty-year-old Dee Dee Moore told semi-illiterate Abraham she was appalled by how he was being fleeced, and offered to become his financial advisor. She offered to help conserve what was left of Abraham's winnings and his assets, and set up a company in Abraham's name, secretly giving herself control of all of Abraham's funds, even his house.

She wasn't looking after Abraham's money so much as spending all of it. She withdrew $1 million, bought expensive cars and went on luxury holidays. After finding out that Dee Dee was rapidly spending all his money and he could do nothing about it, Abraham confronted her and threatened to kill her.

By the end of 2009, Abraham was missing. His family hadn't seen him since April and were worried. Following up on a tip-off, the police searched the back yard of a house purchased by Dee Dee. After digging down 9 feet of dirt under a newly laid concrete slab, they discovered Abraham's body with two bullet holes in the chest. Obviously, Dee Dee was a prime suspect and taken in for questioning. The police interviewer said to Dee Dee: 'Do I think that you're a cold-blooded killer? I hope you're not a cold-blooded killer.' To which Dee Dee replied: 'I have not killed that man.'

Dee Dee's response, as a supposed friend of the victim, is revealing. She uses the distal demonstrative 'that' when she refers to Abraham (along with 'man'). Her language shows distance, an unusual approach given that she was supposed to be Abraham's close friend. By February 2010, Dee Dee was formally charged with Abraham's murder, and sentenced to life imprisonment.

The distal demonstrative can be really useful in revealing lies. Who can forget one of the most infamous lies ever told in modern times, when US President Bill Clinton intoned: 'I did not have sexual relations with that woman.' A quick evaluation of his language reveals indicators to his lying, most notably the distancing language to psychologically separate from the young intern Monica Lewinsky.

The degree to which a person may associate with or distance themselves from a topic in their speech is a form of verbal immediacy[9] – it is part of how we use spatial and temporal terms. When certain types of distancing language are used, it shows avoidant behaviour and encodes a speaker's 'negative affective state'[10] – a subjective experience of a range of negative emotions such as anxiety, anger and envy. Therefore, in unexpected occurrences, if a speaker is using linguistic distance in any of its forms to create space between themselves and something or someone else, we really should be on our guard.

## Changing pronouns

Pronouns belong to a class of words known as function words. Function words are also prepositions, articles and auxiliary verbs. These words (or particles) are mainly very short in length, quickly pronounced and easily missed. A native English speaker has a vocabulary of tens of thousands of words.[11] Even though function words only account for around four hundred of this total, they comprise over half the words used in day-to-day speech.[12]

With function words, linguists also know that there are demographic differences, such as age and gender, in their usage; there is a higher tendency amongst women to use first-person singular pronouns than men,[13] and as we get older, we use fewer first-person singular pronouns and more first-person plural pronouns (we).

Pronoun usage is found to be one of the main features in language which helps to distinguish between truth and lies.[14] This is because our choice of pronouns is another way we can encode distance in language. We create distance by avoiding using the first-person singular pronoun I, separating ourselves from the event or action we are describing. For example, a friend told me about a colleague she used to work with and how when other colleagues who he did not really like were leaving the company, he would write the following type of message: *'You will be missed'*. He did not write: *'I will miss you'*, or any other type of message using the first-person pronoun, and this was because psychologically he was indicating his distance (or dislike) of the leaver and that *he* would not be missing them. The avoidance of using the first-person pronoun can be a prominent indicator of lying, whereas we see immediacy and nearness in a higher use of first-person pronouns, which speakers use more when they are telling the truth.[15]

Five days into their Caribbean holiday, Helen and John were at the beach. Just as they were settling into their sunloungers, John decided he wanted to go for a swim. Not wanting to get her hair wet, Helen decided not to join him but to stay on the beach sunbathing. Knowing that there were strong currents, Helen shouted out to John as he walked towards the sea: 'Be careful! I mean it.' Married for fifteen years, together for over twenty, the couple had met when Helen became John's secretary. But in 2011, Helen was now in her forties and an established and successful author of young adult novels. With hectic and busy lives, the holiday to Barbados was a chance for the couple to de-stress. John had been particularly under pressure at work, although as soon as he arrived in Barbados in February 2011, he was able to relax.

That day, as Helen was enjoying a chat with other holidaymakers, someone shouted out that there was a man in trouble. Quickly, Helen scanned the sea looking for John. He was further out in the ocean; and waving towards the people on the beach. 'He's playing up,' Helen first thought, 'he's being daft.' But John wasn't playing around; he had been swept out by a strong current and was frantically trying to gain the beachgoers' attention. In shock, Helen could only watch while people rushed to form a human chain to get him out of the current. After reaching John, the rescuers brought him back to the beach, pumping his chest to clear his lungs of water. An ambulance arrived, but during the dreadful ride to the hospital, John was knocked off the trolley while the medics were using a defibrillator. Once they were at the hospital and John was taken away, Helen was taken to one side by a doctor, and she knew it was bad. 'He's dead, isn't he?' she said, and the doctor replied: 'I'm so sorry.'

Returning home to the UK, Helen plunged into writing a blog about her experiences as a grieving widow. Her somewhat humorous, frank and emotional accounts became her coping mechanism, and were published in a new book. A few months after John's death, Helen was browsing an online bereavement site, when she started chatting to a middle-aged widower – Ian Stewart. His wife had died suddenly as well, and Helen and Ian struck up a friendship based upon their shared experiences. After a while, their online friendship became more serious. They enjoyed walking Helen's sausage dog Boris, going out for meals and spending time together. Helen thought: 'I don't want to lose this man,' so they decided to sell their respective homes and move in together. Their new house in a small English village was lovely: a large, detached property with grounds and outbuildings. Helen continued her writing as she settled into her new life with Ian.

A few years went by, and Helen started to feel unwell. She didn't know why she was tired all the time – some days she could hardly get out of bed, and her mind was very cloudy. She googled: 'Why do I feel tired all the time?' to no avail. And then, in April 2016, Helen went missing from her home. Ian thought she had wanted to get away for a few days, staying at their seaside home. But she wasn't there. Ian called the police: 'Hello there, my partner has been missing since Monday and not contacted anyone, said she was going away, hasn't gone . . . ended up where she said she was going so I'm, we, we just decided we should report it.'[16]

Ian was lying about Helen's disappearance. He had been secretly feeding her insomnia drugs, had suffocated her, killed poor Boris and hidden both their bodies down a cesspit at their house. All along he'd been after Helen's money. In Ian's call to the police, his deception can be heard when he immediately switches his pronoun use from the non-distant first-person singular I to the more distant we.

Here's another deceptive speaker – the US ex-politician Anthony Weiner. He switches his pronoun use when being asked by a reporter if he had sent 'sexts' and explicit photos of himself to young women:

**Reporter:** 'This is the picture that er I'm sure you've seen it by now. Is this you?'

**Weiner:** 'I can tell you this, we have a firm that we've hired to, I've seen it it's I've seen it, a firm that we've hired to try to get to the bottom of it.'[17]

Weiner insisted that he was the victim of a prank or his Twitter account had been hacked, and strenuously denied that he was the author of these communications. He was interviewed many times on this issue, until the evidence was overwhelmingly against him. He subsequently admitted that he had indeed sent these images and messages.

Why do we find liars switching their pronouns? Primarily, it is used as a way of constructing distance between themselves and their crime or actions. Both Ian Stewart and Anthony Weiner self-correct or switch their usage from the first-person singular pronoun to the first-person plural, which gives us an insight into their lack of prior construction – they hadn't specifically thought through their statements in detail. Therefore, when they use the first-person singular, their intuition feels that it is too revealing or too close, giving 'self-focus', and they switch to the more distant first-person plural 'we' instead without even realising.

When they use we, who is we referring to? Pronouns require a shared knowledge between the speaker and the listener of who it is that they are referring to. The listeners to these transcripts do not know who we refers to (and neither do we). The English pronoun 'we' does not give any information on how many people it refers to apart from 'I and at least one other person'. The listeners may assume that the person speaking is the spokesperson for perhaps not just two people, or three, but maybe a whole group of unidentifiable and unknown people. And by what authority would the listeners disbelieve a whole group of people? In using we, liars are seeking safety in numbers, and hiding within an imaginary collective.

I was once called in to my daughter's school to discuss my daughter apparently bullying another child. This experience will probably resonate with other parents. My daughter's birthday was imminent, and she had invited a large group of friends to her party, but she had not invited one particular child. The child in question did not seem to be bothered, but her mother certainly was. So, the mother lied to the school and claimed that my daughter had called her daughter some derogatory names, which she had been present to hear at the end of the school day. I knew this not to be true as this particular mother was always late to collect her daughter from school, which meant that my daughter would have never been in the playground at the same time as her.

I listened closely as the mother kept switching

pronouns from I to we, by saying things like: 'When I was, we were in the playground,' and: 'I . . . we heard her say it.' Sadly, it wasn't the place in which to give the teacher a linguistics lesson and unfortunately my daughter had to accept an undeserved punishment against my protests. Sometimes, life really is unfair.

## It's all about you

There is a deceptive form of relationship-building interaction where dangerous deceivers change their pronoun use so that the focus is on the listener. This deceptive communication strategy is recognised in the linguistic patterns of romance scammers[18] and sexual predators.[19] These scams are a serious problem: in just a five-year period in the US, $1.5 billion were reportedly lost to romance scammers.[20] These are fraudsters who impersonate someone else; they build fake profiles and contact strangers (usually women and online) with whom they then try to develop a relationship. Over time, they seduce their targets and at some point they will then rob them by creating fake disaster stories and manipulating their target to help them by sending them money. Then they disappear.

Romance scammers and sexual predators try to build intimacy and cultivate a sense of trust in their targets by using more second-person pronouns (you). They will also reduce their use of first-person pronouns (I) to avoid self-disclosure as they do not want to reveal too much about themselves.

Here's a romance scammer displaying that typical deceptive linguistic style:[21]

> 'You know I still love you no matter what I still love you as my wife and I know you gonna be my queen so why worry. Am with you and love in control and nothing more. Trust am with you deeply, because you are the only one I ever love, if am not lying to you. Love is in control trust me I will change your situation and make you happy. You just give me a chance to prove myself. Be with me never ever worry am your husband trust me am with you all the time. I love you so kisses hugs is for you now.'

This lying lothario uses the second-person pronoun thirteen times, whereas his use of the first-person appears six times. Deceptive speakers who focus on another person for personal, financial or sexual gain will have a higher rate of 'you' in their language. They lessen the use of 'I' as part of their self-monitoring.[22] Their self-monitoring involves making sure they create a favourable impression on the listener while also reducing any attentional focus on themselves.[23] A reduction in use of the first-person pronoun also allows the deceiver to create psychological distance from their deception.[24]

## Where's the agent gone?

As well as demonstratives and pronouns, the way a sentence is structured can also encode distance. Firstly, I need to give you a quick understanding of sentence grammar. It won't take long, and it should be painless. Here goes.

English is what is called an SVO language. This means that in a sentence, the subject comes before the verb which comes before the object (SVO stands for Subject, Verb, Object). Sentences in English can be structured where the verbs are in either an active or passive voice. Active-voice sentences typically tell us what a person or thing does, and this person or thing becomes the subject of the sentence. The subject performs the action, and typically comes before the action (verb). The object is who or what receives the action, and typically follows the action (verb). Simply put, in active-voice sentences, the subject performs the action, such as: 'I dropped the baby.' 'I' is the subject, 'dropped' is the verb, 'the baby' is the object. By contrast, in passive-voice sentences, the object is acted upon by the verb and so no subject appears: 'The baby was dropped.'

Passive-voice sentences typically tell us what is done and to whom, but not who or what did it. So when the passive voice is used, it is normally to highlight the object rather than the subject. The passive voice is used when it is unimportant who performed the action – for example: 'The house was destroyed' – or when it is unknown who or what is performing the action: 'The car was stolen.'

The ordering and inclusion of the subject in a sentence is very important for ascribing agency. Research into language and agency finds that the use of the passive voice reduces attributions of responsibility by taking focus away from the doer of the action. If we hear someone say: 'A woman was attacked,' we are more likely to attribute less responsibility to the offender and associatively less harm to the victim.[25] There is no agency in the sentence, so responsibility has been removed. It is commonly found that people who commit violent crimes use the passive-voice construction as a way of misrepresenting their actions, avoiding responsibility, blaming the victim or concealing their activities.[26] A rapist who says: 'All our clothes at one point were taken off,' hides his responsibility (agency) in removing the victim's clothes.[27] I recently saw a report in the news where the UK Metropolitan Police had shot a man's two dogs in the street, and then when the man got upset, they fired a taser at him. Commenting on this incident to the public, the police said that 'a taser was discharged'.[28] Politicians enjoy using the passive to deflect away from proportioning blame. 'Mistakes were made' is a passive that pops up in quite a few politicians' statements. The passive is also found when we are not really sorry: 'Apologies are offered.' It is very clear that sentences which are in the passive voice, rather than the active voice, create distance.[29] In certain occurrences, their use indicates deceptive speech. Reducing agency or removing responsibility is a way of lying by omission. Liars might know the identity of the subject/agent but are being deceptive by omitting it, or perhaps they themselves are the subject/agent and want to remove or reduce their role in the event. In analysing spoken language for indications of deception, we should watch out for the use of the passive voice.

## The position of please

We've seen how sentence structure is an area of language use we should concentrate on for detecting deception, but so is the position in a sentence that speakers will use certain words or phrases like 'please'. In English, the word please is not only used as a politeness marker when we ask for something, but can also be used in a direct or pleading sense. When we plead, we make an emotional or earnest appeal to someone.

The position of please at the end of the sentence, as in: 'Close the door, please,' is used more commonly as a form of politeness.[30] It is rare to find the word please used in an initial position for indirect (polite) requests ('Please, is it possible for you to close the door'), as indirect requests are more likely to position 'please' finally ('Is it possible for you to close the door, please').[31] When we

## HOW TO DETECT LIES OF LITTLE CHANGES

use or encounter please in an initial position, we should consider it as directly demanding an action.[32] This difference in the position of please between demanding action (initial position) and politeness (final position) can help indicate whether a speaker is genuine or perhaps hiding something. A speaker who has had nothing to do with an emergency or event will more likely place please in the action position (initial) when asking for help. Like this innocent caller who uses the word please to demand that the emergency services come to her address when four pit-bull dogs attacked her mother: 'Please, please, just send police to my location right now.'[33] Whereas those speakers who should raise our suspicion in emergency situations are those who use please as a politeness marker in a final position.

Here's a young woman who called 911 after hearing robbers leave her house who had ransacked the property and killed her parents while she hid: 'Help me, please!'[34] she cried to the emergency operator. You might notice that she placed please at the end of the sentence, an indication that perhaps she wasn't telling the whole truth. This is because please occurs in the polite position of the sentence and politeness increases psychological distance.[35] As we know, psychological distance in language use is a good indicator of deception. Being polite in a situation where urgency is expected and politeness is not should get our attention, as an urgent demand should place please at the beginning.

The use of a politeness marker in these instances is a way for the speaker to create distance between themselves and the situation they are involved in. Indeed, the caller in our example had been involved in this crime against her parents. Years of extreme pressure had led her to orchestrate their murder and hire killers to fake a home invasion. Her lies were found out and she, her ex-boyfriend and two other accomplices were all sentenced to life in prison.

Being polite can also be a way of trying to give the false impression by the speaker that they are too nice to be involved in the crime they are calling about. As we have seen, counter-intuitively, swearing or being rude increases the likelihood that a speaker is being genuine in what they are saying – so desperate are they for action and urgency that they have thrown niceties out the window. Remember, there is little time to be polite when the truth is urgently needing to be told.

## Slipping into the past

Lies are not all bad. Certain lies and scams can help raise important social issues, combat prejudice and reveal bias, or might simply offer comedic entertainment. One of the world's greatest hoaxers was Alan Abel. His hoaxes were 'fake news' long before the term became popularised. Throughout the second half of the twentieth century, he successfully duped newspapers, television and radio with satirical pranks.

As it was generally the media who were prey to his pranks, it was probably with some relief that in January 1980 they published his obituary. Alan's widow informed the *New York Times* of his early demise after suffering from a heart attack. Understandably suspicious, the *Times* checked the facts of Alan's death – they contacted the undertaker who had a business listing in the telephone directory; there had been a memorial service in Manhattan and Alan's grieving widow was suitably distressed. This was evidence enough for the *New York Times* to run the obituary:

> *Alan Abel, a writer, musician and film producer who specialized in satire and lampoons, died of a heart attack yesterday at Sundance, a ski resort near Orem, Utah, while investigating a location for a new film. He was 50 years old and lived in Manhattan and Westport, Conn.*

But of course, Alan wasn't dead. It was another one of his hoaxes. He showed up at an organised conference the day after the obituary was printed in the *New York Times*. His hoax was a publicity stunt, he claimed, purely to publicise his professional hoaxing. The media had fallen again for Alan's spoofing, and over the ensuing decades more and more of Alan's hoaxes would find their way into being reported as fact. He was a 'menace to the media'. By

September 2018, Alan got his second (and real) obituary published in the *New York Times*:

> *Alan Abel, a professional hoaxer who for more than half a century gleefully hoodwinked the American public [. . .] apparently actually did die, on Friday, at his home in Southbury, Conn. He was 94.*[36]

In both of Alan's obituaries, he is referred to using the past tense, and this is what we naturally use to refer to a person when they have died. Tense is about time, and communicates when a person did something, or when someone or something existed or happened. Unexpected tense changes can, depending upon the context, also be an indicator of psychological distance,[37] and therefore of intended deception.

Watching out for tense changes from the present to the past is especially important in missing-person appeals. When a person is suspected to be missing, as there is no evidence that they are deceased, we anticipate that the present tense should be used to refer to them. Our knowledge of them is that they are still alive, just missing. But if we hear the past tense being used, this might point to the speaker having knowledge that they are not simply missing.

Let's consider a case about a student called Stephen. He murdered Lauren, another young student he had a fixation on, and hid her dismembered body in rubbish

## HOW TO DETECT LIES OF LITTLE CHANGES

bins. While many people were conducting searches for her, Stephen was interviewed by television journalists. He is asked about her being missing, and he replies: 'Yeah, Lauren was my neighbour . . .'[38] He refers to her in the past tense, yet at the time of the interview, Lauren was only missing. She was still his neighbour, and therefore we would expect him to say instead: 'Yeah, Lauren *is* my neighbour.' His use of the past tense reveals that he has knowledge of her no longer being alive. A clever cop would identify him as a person of interest.

Watch out though – there are some liars who slip in tense changes, so it appears that they are not lying. Have a look at another interview with Bill Clinton. See his reply to the interviewer's question when he is asked about the affair:

**Interviewer:** ' "No improper relationship" – define what you mean by that.'

**Clinton:** 'Well, I think you know what it means. It means that there is not a sexual relationship, an improper sexual relationship, or any other kind of improper relationship.'

**Interviewer:** 'You had no sexual relationship with this young woman?'

**Clinton:** 'There is not a sexual relationship – that is accurate.'[39]

Clinton changed the interviewer's past tense (had) when he answered the question, switching to the present: 'There **is** not a sexual relationship.' Indeed, there wasn't a sexual relationship at the time that Clinton was being interviewed as the affair had ended months before: he did state the truth, but he wasn't answering what the interviewer asked. We would be forgiven for thinking that there was no affair, and in fact many people did. Any tense change, no matter how small, in a speaker's language should demand your lie-detecting attention.

## A different aspect

There's another subtle change that can indicate deception or lies, and this is the aspect. Like tense, grammatical aspect is also to do with time, encoding information on the completion, duration or repetition of an action, event or state, into the verb. Many languages make the distinction between two primary categories of aspect: perfective and imperfective. In simple terms, the past-perfective aspect is used to show the completion of an event – there is no reference to the flow of time (for example, the sentence: 'I waited for him' shows that the wait was not ongoing, it was finite and completed). Whereas the imperfective aspect (as in: 'I was waiting for him') emphasises the ongoing nature of an event. In the English language, imperfective aspect is realised by the past-progressive verb form of -ing verbs (waiting, walking, talking) – and perfective by the use of the simple past-tense verb form – the -ed/t verbs (waited, walked, talked, learned/learnt).

A listener's perception of intentionality can be influenced by differences in these grammatical aspects.[40] Statements about a person's behaviour in the past-perfective aspect ('Will slapped Chris') can make the person appear less responsible for their actions, whereas the imperfective aspect ('Will was slapping Chris') can make the person appear more accountable. With criminal intentionality being a common criterion for legal definitions (first-degree murder, manslaughter etc.), lawyers who present their clients using the past-perfective aspect could reduce the jurors' and court's perceived intentionality of their client.[41] Grammatical aspect is a very important part of language and it can influence judgements and perceptions about other people's behaviour.

Another significant form of aspect is found in the way that we deny our involvement in an event. In these denials, we use one of two grammatical structures: either the present-perfect: 'I have not . . .' or the simple past: 'I did not . . .' These may appear interchangeable but they are, in fact, very different. To understand why, we need to look at the principle of linguistic alignment. This is when two speakers in conversation match or repeat each other's word or sentence choices.[42] When this doesn't happen, we should be on alert. The following crime case will show you how this works.

Could you be charged with the murder of someone if there is no proof that that person is dead, and their body has never been found? Could you still be charged with murder if there are no witnesses or forensic evidence? Surprisingly, the answer is yes. This is what happened to Nicholas Kay. In the early 1990s, Nicholas's wife Rhonda disappeared. The couple had been married for a few years, ran a small business together in the south of England and supplemented their income by renting out rooms in their home to lodgers. Not long into their marriage, Rhonda discovered that Nicholas was having an affair with one of the female lodgers. Although Rhonda seemed to forgive her husband's infidelity, she didn't let him forget it. Nor was she inclined to keep it secret from friends and family, as she frequently told people about his adultery – usually in Nicholas's presence.

It will come as no surprise that the couple were prone to arguments, and it was after one particular argument on the evening of 5 November 1992 that Rhonda stormed out of their house. Returning later in the middle of the night, she found her husband in bed with another lodger. In fury, Rhonda lashed out at the pair of them, ordering the lodger to leave her house. But according to Nicholas, it was Rhonda who apparently left, without taking any clothes, money, bank cards, passport or other possessions. She didn't even drive off in her car. And perhaps most surprising of all, she left behind their young son. She disappeared – never to be seen or heard of again.

As in most cases of a missing person, a public appeal was made. With the police present, reporters were allowed to question Nicholas on his wife's whereabouts. One reporter took a brazen attitude with his questioning, asking Nicholas: 'Did you kill your wife?' Such a direct question is unusual in appeals, and Nicholas was taken aback. He responded to the reporter with: 'What do you think?' But when the reporter told him to: 'Just answer the question,' Nicholas stated: 'No, I haven't killed my wife.'

The police thought otherwise. For eight years they still had no evidence to prove Nicholas was his wife's murderer, so detectives were permitted to install surveillance devices in Nicholas's home: the home he now shared with the lodger Rhonda had found him in bed with.

Instructed by detectives to call Nicholas and lie to him, Rhonda's sister told him that Rhonda's remains had been found, that DNA tests were being done, and that the police were going to get him for her sister's murder. This lie triggered the result the police were after: the surveillance devices recorded Nicholas and his lover referring to a body in a lake, along with other incriminating details. It was on this evidence that Nicholas was convicted for manslaughter and sentenced to six years in prison.

We may think that the two sentences: 'I haven't killed

my wife' and 'I did not kill my wife' are saying the same thing, but there is a difference. In Nicholas's response to the reporter who asks him: 'Did you kill your wife?' he should have linguistically aligned by responding: 'No, I did not kill my wife' – matching his answer with the reporter's question, which is in the past simple.

This is exactly what we find in another convicted murderer's transcript. An Australian, Bradley Murdoch, was sentenced to life imprisonment for the murder of a young man. During his trial, Murdoch was questioned by the prosecution, who said:

> **Prosecution:** 'You murdered Peter Falconio, didn't you?'
>
> **Murdoch:** 'No, I have not.'[43]

We can see how strange the murderer's response is – the question was posed in the past simple and so we'd expect a speaker's answer to align or copy the question, such as: 'No, I did not.'

We also use the past-simple form when we want to indicate that something is over and done with ('I did not kill my wife'), but both killers use the present-perfect form, which implies that an action is still ongoing ('I have not killed my wife'). This may seem a little obscure, but stay with me. We can see the difference between these two sentences in how they relate to time if we put the word yet at the end. With: 'I did not kill my wife yet', the sentence becomes ungrammatical, indicating how the past-simple form signals that an action is left in the past. Whereas: 'I have not killed my wife yet' works perfectly well when an action is not completed. But this action is really one about the liar and killer, in this case Nicholas, who has not yet been found out. So, in a way, his sentence here can be heard as: 'I have not killed my wife [as you have no proof yet].'

We find this same tense and aspect usage in the partner of a murdered young mother, who denied killing her, although he was later convicted. 'I have not killed Natalie,' he says. 'I have not hurt Natalie. I did tell you this in the previous interview.'[44] Notice how he changes from the present perfect when asserting he wasn't the killer or responsible for hurting her, to the past simple when stating he had said this already to the police. Even when murderers emphatically deny murdering or killing someone, the use of the present perfect often appears in their speech.

Does this mean that when we hear the past simple being used, it increases the likelihood that the speaker is telling the truth? Perhaps so, although we should be aware that it isn't as clear-cut as that, and we should have a comprehensive look. Going back to Dee Dee Moore, for example, and her declaration that: 'I have not killed that man,' there are three separate occurrences of language use that increase the probability of her lying: (1) she uses the present perfect: 'I have not killed,' (2) she uses distance with the distal demonstrative 'that', and (3) she further distances herself when she refers to Abraham, who was meant to be her friend, as 'man' rather than by his name.

Let me quickly expand upon that principle of conversation, 'linguistic alignment', which I introduced to you earlier in this section. When we interact with others, we have a tendency to mimic their behaviour, and they mimic ours. This mimicry takes place not only with physical actions (like body language)[45] but also speech.[46] This is what linguistic alignment is and it is a common feature between conversational partners.[47] This alignment can occur whereby partners start patterning with the same words, sentence constructions and conceptual areas. Any one of these features used by one conversational partner can elicit a similar representation in the other. As we've seen, an accusatory style of questioning such as: 'Did you kill your wife?' should of course elicit the short-denial response of: 'No, I did not,' which results in no discernible way of differentiating the language use of a liar or a truth-teller. However, we should not be too quick to discard short-denial responses, as those that do not align with an accusatory question can be a cue to deception. This is what we have seen in those liars not aligning with the sentence grammar of the question asked of them. We do indeed find that decreasing alignment or mimicry should be looked at closely as it can indeed be an indicator of deception.[48]

## Simply lies

Wendy's is one of the biggest fast-food chains in the US. Back in March 2005, Anna, a forty-year-old American woman, and her husband decided to visit one of the Wendy's restaurants in San Jose, California. Halfway through eating her bowl of chilli, Anna bit into something unusual and quickly spat it out. Upon closer examination, Anna realised it was a severed human finger.

Anna ran up to other customers to warn them not to eat their food, showing them what she had found in hers. The restaurant's customers, staff and managers were shocked and disgusted by Anna's find. The Environmental Health team was informed, and when they arrived, they started checking all the employees' hands in case one of them had (strangely) chopped their finger off while preparing the food! 'We asked everybody to show us they have ten fingers and everything is OK there,' said the director. They wanted to see if the finger could be traced back to the manufacturer, but after a thorough investigation and contacting the suppliers it was concluded that the finger didn't come from any Wendy's employee or their suppliers.

The police were called to help with the investigation, and news of Anna's grisly find started to spread rapidly. Wendy's released a statement trying to mitigate the awful publicity, claiming: 'Food safety is of utmost importance to us.' But word got around, and people avoided eating at Wendy's. The fast-food chain lost $2.5 million in revenue, and dozens of employees were laid off. As this grisly incident gained more attention, investigators started to think that maybe Anna had planted the finger in her chilli. For one, there were no teeth marks on the finger, though Anna claimed that she had bitten into it.

The investigators were right, and Anna had indeed planted the offending digit in her chilli. Whose finger was it? The police eventually found out that the finger belonged to an associate of Anna's husband. This man had sold his finger to Anna to settle a debt after losing it in an industrial accident. More shocking still, this was not the first time that Anna had pulled a stunt like this: she had a history of filing fraudulent lawsuits. But this time, Anna and her husband wound up in prison, serving many years for the finger fraud.

Before her fraud was uncovered, Anna appeared on a national news programme to describe the moment she found the finger:

> 'Well, as I was eating my chilli . . . and er . . . I usually just crack all my crackers and put them in there, mix it all around, and started eating, eating and eating the way people usually eat huh and suddenly I er chew something that's kinda hard, crunchy. Spit it out. At first, I wasn't sure what it was. And er so we started investigating by poking it. Other people too. That's

when we find that there's something that looks like a nail. There are no words to describe what I felt, what was going through me. I mean, it is something that's [long pause] my God, it is sick.'[49]

Apart from having minimal sensory-perceptual details, Anna's description of her gruesome find is told in very simplistic terms. Deceptive speakers are found to avoid sentence structures with difficult syntactic composition, where there are a higher number of words before the main verb of the main clause.[50] For example, if Anna's finger story were not invented, she might have said something like: 'I wasn't sure what it was, so I spat it out.' The main clause here is: 'I spat it out' and there are many words before the main verb 'spat'. This would make this sentence syntactically difficult. But Anna uses simplistic phrases with the absence of words before the main verb – 'spit it out', and no verbs – 'other people too'. There is no syntactic complexity in Anna's story at all. Her story is so simplistic that she does not include adjectives to describe how she felt, and she even tells us there are no words to describe how she felt!

When lies are constructed, there will be cognitive strain which can result in the simplification of sentences.[51] A liar will endure an increased cognitive load when maintaining a lie, so it is expected that they will reduce the cognitive load of more complex sentence constructions by using more simpler options.[52] It is harder for them to produce linguistically complex language.[53] We should also find that as lies themselves become more complex, then sentence complexity will further reduce.

Psychological research suggests that cognitive strain does affect the complexity of language and therefore brief or simplistic sentences or utterances that use fewer words are found to be associated with deception.[54] Deceptive speakers will avoid inconsistency by providing fewer details in case they have to retell their lies,[55] so simplifying what is said is safer.

Of course, we expect that sentence complexity will increase and decrease throughout the telling of a story, but we should be alert to the moments when it does decrease. It could signify that this is the part of the narrative which is key to determining deception.

## Telling it like it happened

We are now going to look at the 'big picture' – the full story of what a speaker says. Normally, our stories are a description of events in the chronological order in which they happened. A story has a beginning, a middle and an end – 'a sequence of events'.[56] There is a common structure to oral stories: orientation – which is setting the scene; complication – what happened; evaluation – the narrator's opinion; resolution – the outcome; and the coda – the narrator returns to the present time.[57] Stories won't always include every section of this common structure, but do generally follow the temporal sequencing of events. If they don't, it affects how we comprehend, understand and recall these stories.[58]

Let's see how this normally works in a truthful account from a man who has been blind since birth. He describes a true and frightening experience:

> 'I've got a reclining chair and I was laying in that listening to some music and all at once I heard two crashes in the bathroom so five minutes after I thought things might have blown over in the wind and five minutes after I went to pick 'em all up and I found this "carpety" thing on the bathroom floor [. . .] well, it was like a "carpety" sort of thing on the floor I thought some insulation had come adrift or something so I picked all the bottles up that that had fallen over and I went a few paces a few steps forward to try and pick this thing up – couldn't – too heavy. It was too too heavy to lift. So, I rang the office, I'm in supported living you see I rang the office you see and I said to the staff member: "Can you pop over I think I've got a mess in my bathroom?" So, Jason one of my support workers came over, walked in the bathroom, took one short glance down and said: "You've got a snake in your bathroom." [. . .] well, I've heard it came out through the loo, through the toilet.'[59]

The snake was an eight-foot python!

We see how this man's oral narrative follows the typical structure of a story. The chronological sequencing of 'as it happened' is familiar and typical to a story's structure. The speaker sets the scene: 'I was laying in that listening to some music'; explains what happened: 'I heard two crashes'; offers his opinion: 'I thought some insulation had come adrift or something'; provides a resolution: 'you've got a snake in your bathroom'; and returns to the present time: 'well, I've heard it came out through the loo'. Note also how he uses sensory language in 'carpety' and 'too heavy to lift'. The effect is that we believe the speaker – and indeed, he is telling the truth.

If there are changes or alterations to the temporal sequencing of a story, it not only affects how we comprehend or remember what is said, it also affects our perception of whether the story is true or not. A story or narrative where the temporal sequencing is random or altered leads people to assume that the story must be implausible or deceptive, although truth-tellers are more likely to give accounts which are sometimes unstructured.[60] Without prompting, we return to earlier parts of our narrative to fill in extra details that we suddenly remember or that we think are relevant. When we lie, on the other hand, we find it a lot harder to remove ourselves from the sequence of events and will usually just give a basic structure. We construct our lies on a time-plan – what happened next – whereas when we tell the truth, we can go back to earlier parts of our narrative as we are recalling what happened, not inventing it.

This is why in the snake in the bathroom account, the blind man returns to fill in an extra detail: 'I'm in supported living you see.' One technique used by interviewers to draw out liars is to ask the speaker to re-tell their narrative backwards (we will look at this later on in more detail). This task puts more cognitive load on the speaker, so when liars must re-tell their lies in reverse order, they often get themselves confused, as their invented ordered sequence has changed. This re-telling of lies results in them revealing other indicators of deception, such as their speech becoming slower, or with a greater number of speech errors and hesitations (which we will look at soon) and less descriptive detail.[61]

## The length of lies

Commonly, as we have seen, lies are often shorter and contain less detail than truthful answers.[62] Intuitively, we seem to be aware of this as we believe that truthful answers involve greater detail than lies.[63] Another possible reason why a speaker's lies have a shorter duration in length is that the liar is hesitant to offer more information than necessary, as by doing so they are likely to reveal incriminating evidence.

We also find that there is a variation in length between lies which are prepared and those that aren't. As explained earlier, in prepared lies – where liars have had a chance to plan what they say – most often their lies will be longer than those of unprepared liars. Planned deception is indicated by the use of more unnecessary words and sentences – speaking for longer or loquaciousness.[64] This is why an analysis of duration should be considered in tandem with the content of what is being said. Truth-tellers will be more specific about details like place and time. As we know, they appear to include words that relate to the senses (sensory-perceptual words), details which a liar will be less likely to include.[65] On the other hand, liars will go into greater detail in unnecessary sections (like the spies and the exact measurement of Salisbury Cathedral's spire) and will shorten or skip over crucial details.

See whether you think our next speaker is being deceptive or not in his account of being attacked.

A young black American TV star was opening his mail one morning in January 2019, when he couldn't believe what someone had sent him. On the page of a letter, the sender had drawn a stick figure hanging from a tree with a gun pointing towards it. It said: 'You will die.' The acronym MAGA had also been scrawled on the letter, a reference to President Trump's electioneering slogan: 'Make America Great Again.' Jussie was worried. He should have been, as he was attacked a few days later

## HOW TO DETECT LIES OF LITTLE CHANGES

while leaving his hotel room in the early hours of the morning in Chicago. Two weeks after the assault, ABC TV channel interviewed Jussie about the attack; this is his account of what happened:

> 'When I landed in Chicago and Frank Gatson who's like my uncle and he's also my creative director and he picked me up and then we got back to the apartment and there was no food and so I went out to Walgreens thinking that they were twenty-four hours and to have a smoke er Walgreens was closed um so I called him up and I said hey I'm gonna run to Subway which was across the street and I'm gonna get a salad – do you want anything? I went to the Subway and got the order during that time I texted my manager thinking that he was still in Australia because he was on an Australian tour with one of his other clients. I said you know call me when you can and he called me immediately and while he was on the phone I er heard as I was crossing the intersection, I heard "Empire" and I don't answer to "Empire", my name ain't "Empire" er and I didn't answer I kept walking and then I heard "n***** Empire n*****" so I turned around and I said you just say to me? And I see ... the attacker ... masked.'

Phew! Did you see that there's an awful lot of information that Jussie supplies leading up to the attack?

As we saw earlier, a truthful recall of experienced events has three parts to a narrated incident – an account of what happened before, during and after the incident.[66] In deceptive accounts, there may be unnecessary lengthening of what happened leading up to the incident (before), with fewer details or less information given about the actual incident (during) as this is where the lies are. Let's go back to Jussie and see how he carries on with the crucial part of his story:

> 'And he said "this is MAGA country n*****" and punches me right in the face so I punched his ass back and then um we started tussling you know it was very icy and we ended up tussling by the stairs er fighting, fighting, fighting. There was a second person involved who was kicking me in my back and er then it just stopped.'[67]

There's a clear lack of detail and much brevity in the crucial part of Jussie's story compared to the events leading to the attack. A reduction in the length of their description during the incident may be a way for a liar to hide that they are making it up. With Jussie's story, the overly long explanation of what happened before the attack and the reduced explanation of the attack itself give a good indication that things are not what they seem. This lack of detail is a way in which liars will also hide their involvement in an incident or crime, or skip over other details that may implicate them.

Have a look at the following deceptive account of a woman who, along with an accomplice, murdered her lover's partner. In her interview, the police are trying to establish where she was on the day of the murder. The police are certain she carried out the murder as her accomplice has already confessed to their involvement:

> **Police:** 'Fourteenth of January this year, Thursday just gone, where were you?'
>
> **Williams:** 'I was at home in Chester, I got home at [pause] I think about four. David met me at the house erm I'd been sent home from work with a sickness [pause] bug then he went home [pause] and then I went to sleep. I woke up the first time at maybe [protracted] nine-ish but that was the dog that woke me up barking, and that's what I did I wiped up some dog-sick . . .'[68]

Notice how she does not just state where she was: 'I was at work then I was at home,' but gives plenty of information (from 4 p.m.) and then claims she was asleep but wakes up at the most crucial time – 9 p.m., the time of the murder. She then continues with more information. She omits the 'during' section of her narrative by claiming to be asleep. Taking notice of the length of a speaker's story, which parts are longer and which are shorter, is also a useful approach in separating truth from lies.[69]

A liar's story can often be quite simplistic in language, and they will try to skip over the parts that they are attempting to hide. It's important to note that this can happen even when their re-telling of the events leading up to the crucial incident are verbose and detailed. A liar will also commonly recount something in a chronological timeframe, whereas a truth-teller is more likely to return to earlier parts to include details that they may have missed out. As psychological distance is encoded in language through using distal demonstratives, switching pronouns and through certain tense and aspect structures, being alert to these small shifts that signal unexpected distance may help in detecting a fabricated story as well.

But what about the parts of language that aren't as clear-cut as the words we use, and the order we use them in? What about *how* liars tell lies? That's what's known as the paraverbal, and it encodes a great deal of useful information for lie detection too.

CHAPTER 3

# Paraverbal: How to detect lies in vocal cues

When we speak, it's not only lexical and grammatical words that can indicate if we may be lying, but also the *way* that we speak. In linguistics, the way that we speak is referred to as the paraverbal or paralinguistic: those features of language that communicate information without using any words at all. As soon as we speak, we give away a huge amount of information through the tone of our voice, our accent, our pitch, our volume, how long it takes for us to speak, pauses and silence, 'um's and 'er's and other space fillers, and any speech errors, self-corrections and stumbling.

All these paraverbal indicators are carriers of meaning and are particularly important for lie detection, as how we say something is much harder for us to control or manipulate than the words or grammar we use. However, it can be equally hard for us as listeners to notice paraverbal indicators. This is because our brains naturally filter out much of this information. But if we learn to focus on what a speaker says as well as the way that they say it, it can effectively set us up for detecting deception.[1]

## Highs and lows

One area of my academic research is investigating the use of language in individuals who claim to be possessed by some spirit entity. I'm interested in finding out whether these individuals' language use varies between when they are in a possessed state and when they are not. I also want to discover and examine what they say and how they say it to find out whether there are distinct alterations in their language which may indicate that another personality or entity really has possessed them or whether they are impersonating being possessed. While my research topic may seem a bit strange, it has relevance in that there are incidences of crime, such as murder, where being possessed by a spirit is given as mitigation.[2]

There are a few places in London where exorcism rituals are performed openly, such as in Pentecostal churches, and I occasionally visit these to conduct some of my research. A few years back, I attended one of these exorcism rituals performed in a London Pentecostal church. The congregation was made up of women and men of all ages, and from many different cultural backgrounds.

## HOW TO DETECT LIES IN VOCAL CUES

At a certain point in the day-long service, attendees who believe they have a spirit possessing them are asked to come forward, where they stand in a line and are interviewed by a member of the church as to the nature of their possession. After describing how the possession afflicts their lives, these individuals are prayed over which compels the possessing spirit to appear, taking over the personality of the individual. When within a state of possession, these individuals are interviewed again by the church's officiant. It is these interviews that I closely analyse and I contrast them to what the individuals said before they went into their temporary state of possession.

While I watched and listened, one middle-aged woman who was being interviewed stood out. She described how being possessed by a spirit had caused her marriage to break down; she had lost her job and suffered from feelings of inadequacy and depression. She spoke normally and answered the questions with clarity, complexity and full of details. However, after she was prayed over and the spirit entity that possessed her appeared, when asked questions this spirit answered in a very high-pitched voice. This voice was completely different in pitch from the voice that the woman used when not possessed. Apparently, the spirit that possessed her was a young child. As this spirit answered the questions posed by the church officiant, I listened for key linguistic indicators that it was a child talking.

But there weren't any.

There was a complete mismatch between the high, childlike pitch of this spirit's voice and the things that they said. While the voice appeared to be that of a young child about the age of four or five years old, the structure of the sentences and the words used were those not of a child but of an adult. For example, the possessing spirit said things like: 'Look, I've had enough of this now,' and: 'She's a whore, that's why she's divorced.'

In childhood language development, there are clear milestones for lexical and syntactical acquisition, such as producing new vocabulary (for example, a five-year-old English-speaking child has a spoken vocabulary of roughly 4,000–5,000 words)[3] and using words appropriately along with constructions of sentences which range from simple to complex.[4] Either the possessed woman was fabricating her spirit entity and impersonating a child's voice, or this child spirit had an advanced command of language. I concluded that it was most likely the former.

There is so much we can tell about a person just from the sound of their voice, such as gender and age. Children's voices are well known to be much higher than adult voices; in fact, studies which have measured these differences have concluded that a five-year-old's pitch range will be generally 50 per cent higher than a male adult.[5]

Voice pitch defines the perception of how 'high' or

'low' a person's voice sounds. The pitch of our voices is measured or defined by the rate of vibration of our vocal folds. If the rate of vibration increases per second, then this increases the pitch of our voices to become higher, whereas slower vibrations result in lowered pitch. Atypical vocalisations cover monotonic speech patterns where there is no variation in tone, pitch or speed and the voice will sound robotic with an absence of emotion, irregular intonation, repeated words or phrases, and abnormal voice pitch modulations where a voice may sound too high or low for the age or gender of an individual.

The sound and pitch of an individual's voice also gives indications of emotional states. Expressions of disgust, shame and sadness are encoded with a low pitch, whereas joy, surprise, enthusiasm, anger and happiness have a higher pitch.[6] Think about how your own pitch modulation changes when you are expressing different emotions like annoyance (low pitch), frustration (low pitch) or pleasure (higher pitch). This is the connection between how our internal emotional state is conveyed through our vocal pitch. Think about how you know someone's emotional state through their voice pitch as well. We do this intuitively. Our detection of emotion in pitch is also affective across languages as we can infer the emotional state of a speaker from their pitch even if we cannot understand the language being spoken.[7] When there is a lack of pitch modulation it can also be suggestive of autism spectrum disorder,[8] and psychological states such as schizophrenia and clinical depression.[9]

Let me explain how research is conducted into this finding, but first I need to give you a quick outline of how sound, in particular pitch, is produced.

We produce voice pitch through the frequency of vibrations from the larynx, commonly known as the voice box, which is used in the production of sound. Most of the sounds of the world's languages are produced through something called pulmonic egressive airflow – air passes from the lungs, up the trachea (windpipe), through the larynx and out of either the mouth or the nose. It is within the larynx that the vocal cords, or folds, are situated. These folds are two bands of smooth muscle tissue which can be stiffened to vibrate, and when they do so at a very fast rate it increases the pitch of someone's voice, whereas a slower vibration rate will decrease voice pitch. We can all modulate this vibration rate to vary our pitch range when we speak, although research finds that this appears harder to achieve for individuals with schizophrenia or depression[10] due to cognitive impairment.[11]

This difference in voice pitch is verified through experiments such as one which was a spontaneous speech analysis of three groups of participants with major depressive disorder, schizophrenia spectrum disorder and a healthy control group. These groups were given a picture description task where they were asked to describe the same pictures, express their thoughts and to tell a story of each picture for three minutes. Their speech is recorded and examined, looking at specific speech features using computed models and statistical calculations. Researchers found that the depressive and schizophrenia groups produced differences in speech patterns with less pitch modulation in contrast to the healthy control group, and that speech patterns such as pitch modulation are potential biomarkers to identify psychiatric disorders.[12]

Research into speech and voice pitch finds that indicators of psychiatric and personality disorders are not only found in how an individual speaks but also in how they perceive the speech of others as well. Some studies suggest that an inability to detect emotional signals in voice pitch is associated with psychopathy.[13] We are finding out much more about the importance of voice pitch such as how it can influence our perception of others. Research into the perception of voice pitch has tested participants' judgements of different attributes by listening to a selection of voice samples. These studies find that men who have lower-pitched voices are perceived as physically stronger,[14] more attractive[15] and socially dominant.[16] Other research has found that women who have higher-pitched voices are preferred by men.[17] Research also finds that we make judgements on others' personality characteristics based on their voice pitch. Generally, people with lower pitched voices are more likely to be judged by listeners as having positive personality characteristics than those with higher pitched voices.[18] Personality traits such as intelligence and trustworthiness are ascribed more to individuals with lower-pitched voices, including women.[19] This explains why entrepreneur Elizabeth Holmes famously spoke in a very distinctive, deep voice pitch. Many have made the case that this was probably affected to appear trustworthy when she was far from it; Holmes made many false claims about her company Theranos, defrauding investors of nearly a billion dollars.

Pitch is so important for communicating information that it can sometimes be more reliable than the words which are said. For example, the generally innocuous way of saying we are fine, but in a lower-than-normal pitch, indicates that we are not fine. Who hasn't experienced the common retort from their partner when you ask them: 'What's wrong?' only to be told: 'Nothing,' although their voice pitch clearly indicates that something is wrong. If we want to be better at spotting the indicators of deception in language, we need to pay attention to any pitch variance when a speaker talks, particularly if it contradicts *what* they are saying.

When I was a child, my mother was the best lie detector. I never understood how she was able to spot when I or my two brothers were lying. She always said she knew because our voices 'went up'. I didn't understand what she meant, and given that lying was my brothers' speciality, I thought it was something to do with my brothers' voices. But what my mother was detecting was a change in our pitch range. Even though children generally have a higher pitch than adults, my mother was adept at detecting when our pitch became elevated, and knew that it meant that her children were lying to her. Academic research now confirms what my mother knew forty years ago: there is a substantial increase in pitch when individuals are being deceptive.[20] Stressful situations tend to increase our pitch, and as lying heightens our stress response, this may explain our increase in pitch when we are being deceptive.

You may ask why would stress increase our pitch? This is explained by something called the vagus nerve. The vagus nerve receives information from our brain, lungs, heart and digestive system, and is part of our sympathetic nervous system – our fight-or-flight response. This nerve has two branches; one which sends signals to our vocal folds for opening and closing (the recurrent laryngeal nerve) and a second one (the superior laryngeal nerve) which takes information from the larynx to the brain and controls voice pitch. As lying induces stress, which initiates our sympathetic nervous system, the vocal cords will tense (as will most muscles in our body when the sympathetic nervous system is activated) and increase the vibration rate (and therefore pitch) similarly with increases in heart and breathing rate.[21]

Pitch also becomes higher when we are doubtful or

lack confidence in what we are saying.[22] This can also be related to lying and deception, as if speakers are unsure about how their lies will be received; whether they will be believed or not will cause them to reduce their confidence in what they say. Listening out for increased pitch in a speaker's language can help us with detecting deceit, especially if we are familiar with their normal speaking pitch.

## Sounds nasty

The online advert was posted by Amy, an Arizona mother looking for carers for her Down Syndrome son. Amy explained that even though her son, Paul, was an adult, his disability meant that he needed help with showering, grooming, going to the bathroom and changing diapers. Amy was looking for female caregivers who would be able to deal with Paul's personal needs, and luckily for her, three carers responded to her advert. This was great news. Amy organised paying the carers and communicated with them by text messages. When could they start? Could they pick up her son from these different addresses in a town near Phoenix, Arizona? Paul would be waiting for them: he was thirty years old with dark hair, chubby cheeks and large brown eyes. Even though Amy wasn't available to meet the carers, she trusted them to look after her son, to be discreet and to deal professionally with the intimate nature of his care.

Over the course of nine months, three different female carers would meet Paul and help him bathe and change his diapers. Sometimes Paul would be out on his own at a restaurant or coffee shop and would need the help of one of his carers to take him to a public bathroom to wash him. But what started to worry his carers was that when they were washing Paul in intimate areas, or changing his diaper, he would often get an erection. The carers tried to not let it faze them and carried on professionally looking after their client. Over time, Paul became quite aggressive with them, demanding that they clean his genital area better and 'more thoroughly'. 'He would act in tantrums, talk like a child, act like a child,' complained one carer about Paul's behaviour.

One carer decided that something really wasn't right, but because Amy was never around when the carers were with Paul, they couldn't raise their concerns with her. Eventually one of the carers decided to follow Paul to an unfamiliar address. Driving up to a large grey-and-beige painted house with a perfectly tended garden, Paul's carer watched as he put a key in the door and went inside. She parked her car, got out, walked up the path and knocked on the front door. A man and a woman opened the door, and helpfully answered the carer's questions. Yes, they were Paul's parents, but no, Paul's mother had never placed an advert for a carer, and no, of course he didn't have Down Syndrome and he definitely didn't wear diapers either. Paul was rumbled.

Quickly after meeting his parents, the carer contacted the police who arrested Paul and charged him with sexual abuse and fraud. At his court appearance, Paul declared to the judge: 'I just want to let you know, I am special needs.' Paul had decided the best way of meeting those needs was to pretend to have Down Syndrome to get women to wash and touch his genitals.

Paul's way of impersonating someone with Down Syndrome was to change his voice quality to talk like a child. But if Paul's carers knew anything about it, they would have known that speaking in a child's voice does not typify an adult with Down Syndrome. In fact, adults with Down Syndrome have a voice quality which is generally described as husky, nasal or monotonous, and nowhere near being perceived as childlike.[23] Paul's faked voice quality should have given him away immediately.

Voice quality covers acoustic behaviour such as resonance (the modification of sound which is determined by the shape and size of each of our vocal tracts and nasal cavities), breathiness (incomplete closure of the vocal folds allowing more air to escape when we speak), nasality (the balance of oral and nasal tone in our speech), and of course a speaker's own physiological voice production. Any area of vocal quality can be affected by things such as developmental disorders, psychological state or illness – like how a bad cold can make our voices more nasalised. But vocal quality can also point to deceptive speech.[24] There may be an increase in vocal cord tension, making a liar's voice sound audibly strained, with breaths being taken at odd moments, causing their voice to sound unrelaxed. When a speaker's voice is strained or unrelaxed in this way it is because the stress of lying causes deception-induced arousal.

Voice quality also includes a trembly or shaky voice, which can often arise when a speaker is highly nervous, again due to the vagus nerve. This trembling voice quality is clearly heard in recordings of an interview with the famous US football coach Jerry Sandusky. The interviewer asked him if he had sexually abused young boys, and we can hear Sandusky's voice tremble and quiver in his denials. He is currently in prison having been convicted of serial child molestation.[25]

A few years ago, I had to informally interview one of my students as there was a suspicion of plagiarism in their work. I liked this student and did not want to see them lose their place at university, so I invited him for an informal chat where I asked him about life in general and how his studies were going. I focused on his speech as it flowed naturally, which is key to getting a baseline of someone's voice quality. When I asked this student to talk about their essay (without mentioning any suspected plagiarism), he started to exhibit something called Globus Hystericus. This is the technical term for a lump in your throat: a phantom feeling which affects your voice quality and makes you want to clear your throat with a short cough. It is a known symptom of anxiety, so hearing it in my student raised my suspicion and I thought it best to pursue a formal investigation. Unfortunately, he was indeed found to have cheated.

Being alert to such slight changes in vocal quality is a helpful tool in analysing the speech of liars, if you develop the capacity to listen out for it.

## Slow, slow, quick, quick, slow

The police in Birmingham were worried. All officers serving in the West Midlands police force had to phone in to report that they had got home safely. Even though the national terrorism threat level was severe in the UK, these heightened security measures were unprecedented in 2014. As the Assistant Chief Constable said: 'Never before have we had to instruct officers to call in after their tour of duty to let us know they returned home safely.' Such was the level of fear that an off-duty officer who did not answer an emergency rollcall had an armed response unit turn up at his house. West Midlands police force even put a hostage negotiator on standby. Fear and anxiety were widespread. This was the anonymous phone call that had put everyone on heightened alert, warning that a terrorist was planning to kidnap a Muslim police officer:

## HOW TO DETECT LIES IN VOCAL CUES

**Operator:** 'They are going to kidnap a police officer from Birmingham was it?'

**Caller:** [very fast] 'From from from Birmingham yes, he is saying Birmingham but I don't know if is going to be the West Midlands or not, because at the moment this Irfan is living in Walsall and he is working in a car wash or tyre shop or garage of some sort, called sergeant, sergeant, er . . .'

**Operator:** 'You are going too fast you are going to have to give me a second, OK. So, you have been asked to drive the car?'[26]

The caller had a grudge against the man he describes as a terrorist, and planned to have him arrested on terrorism charges. The caller was actually a West Midlands police officer, who was later jailed for nine years for sparking the terrorism alert.

This caller has such an increased speech rate that the operator has to tell him to slow down. His rapid speech indicates that he has planned or prepared his lies, and speech rate can increase when liars want to move past their section of deceptive speech.[27] There is an emotional response when speakers lie as they could be fearful their lies will be found out, or they might be excited by their lies. An increase in the rate of speech is indicative of this anxiety, stress or excitement. Any variation in speech rate which deviates from our normal rate of speaking can be a sign of deception, especially if it appears at certain sections of a story. However, our speech rate can also significantly decrease when we lie (as it does, naturally, when we age).[28] This is because the cognitive load that is required for lying affects our pace of speaking and slows us down. This can be seen more clearly in cases of unplanned or spontaneous lying, which require on-the-spot thinking about many things at the same time: how to construct the story, word choice, how to frame everything, while also being alert to the reaction of the listener. A reduced speech rate also gives us more time to remember what we are saying in case we get questioned about it later.[29]

Speech rate is usually measured by counting the number of words or syllables spoken per second in a sample and then dividing by the acoustic length of the sample in seconds. We can learn how to detect these changes in speaking rate by getting a baseline of a person's normal rate of speech, and then keeping an ear out for any speed changes when they reach the specific topic that you are concerned about. Decreases in the rate of speaking might indicate that the speaker is closely monitoring what they are saying and the task of lying is mentally taxing, whereas increases in the rate of speaking could be an indication of planned deception alongside emotional arousal.

## I wouldn't hurt a fly

As an undergraduate student, I had a part-time job where I worked with this girl who I could not stand. She was a bully and a really nasty individual. She made my life difficult and would say awful things in a patronising tone to me when no one else was around. At one point, I'd had enough and told our manager, and she was called in to respond to my allegations. When questioned, she denied everything, dropping her voice intensity and using a sweet little girl's voice, softly spoken and melodic. I was astounded. This was not her voice. She used a fake voice, adopting the voice of someone who could not possibly be so horrible. Our manager believed her. I left soon after, but I learnt my lesson: watch out when a speaker drops their vocal intensity.

The intensity or loudness of an individual's voice can act as an indicator of deceptive speech.[30] We often encounter decreased intensity in the speech of someone being deceptive when there is a higher cognitive load on them. As they have to really think about their lies, they become more tentative in what they are saying. A liar might also purposefully reduce their voice intensity as a way of conveying politeness[31] and act as if they are being helpful and respectful. This is a form of impression management. We all do this – manipulate information about ourselves so we are perceived in the way we want others to see us.[32] Deceivers are no different. They want to portray themselves in the best light possible as honest, truth-telling individuals and are more likely to give the appearance that they are amenable and may lower their voice intensity to reflect this. However, this in itself isn't a sure-fire sign of deception: if someone is fearful of authority, for whatever reason, then they may also lower their voice intensity.

When I research videos of real-life instances of high-stakes liars, many show a striking reduction in voice intensity particularly when they state the negator 'no'. If a liar is trying to conceal their character in some way – like they are prone to violence or have a violent or aggressive nature – this decrease is a way of portraying a different persona, a timid, soft or easy-going one which does not fit with the crime or incident that they are being asked about.

Having said that, we should also be on the lookout for an increase in loudness as some liars will attempt to make their voice sound more expressive to give the impression of confidence and believability.[33] Similarly, the stress of lying might increase someone's voice intensity – as could an honest person feeling worried that what they are saying won't be believed.

Some people do naturally have loud voices and some others have quiet voices. But we all mostly speak at accepted volume levels in any social setting. You can train your ears to listen out for changes to the volume (or pitch) of voices in different settings. Voice volume is naturally altered in different environments; we generally speak a bit more quietly in a museum, gallery or place of worship than we would in a pub or bar. So, remember that the setting influences our natural voice volume. Once you are more familiar with recognising volume changes in voices, you can try using voice intensity as a deception detection tool. Firstly, consider the setting, then get a baseline of the other person's voice volume by talking about something unimportant and unemotive like how their day was. Once you have a normal conversation flowing, then move to the topic that you are suspicious of and listen out for any changes to the speaker's normal vocal level or pitch. The key to considering voice intensity as a deception detection tool is to pay attention to any changes to the speaker's normal vocal level and at what point in what they are saying.

## The sounds we don't hear

Abel lived in a small town outside of Detroit. A middle-aged and rotund man, with glasses and tattooed arms, Abel was a member of the large Hispanic community in the area. He didn't live too far from the Weston post office, into which on the morning of 7 December 2009 an armed man entered, ordering that the young, female cashier – Amy Fox – hand over all the money. Terrified, Amy complied, then rang 911 This is her call:

**Operator:** '911.'

**Fox:** 'Um yes this is the Weston Post Office. Someone just robbed me, I need someone out here right now.'

**Operator:** 'Could you tell what kind of weapon he had.'

**Fox:** 'Umm, it was black and it was small . . . so I don't know. It was a handgun.'

**Operator:** 'Can you describe him at all?'

**Fox:** 'Umm he was he had a mask on. He was big. I don't know, um maybe black or Mexican. I don't know if he was Spanish or if he was like African-American and light skinned.'[34]

Amy's account of the robber led the police to Abel, who seemed to fit the description. Questioned for over an hour, Abel was very anxious – he hadn't committed the robbery, but the police thought he had. Why? For no reason other than that he was big and Hispanic-looking. People in the community were on high alert, shocked by the robbery. This was one of those small towns where things like this didn't happen. Abel was concerned that in his close-knit community, people would find out that the police suspected him of the robbery and would judge and exclude him.

## HOW TO DETECT LIES IN VOCAL CUES

Abel had to live under the air of suspicion for some time, until one evening he turned on the news and discovered that Amy Fox had been arrested for the robbery. Postal inspectors conducted a forensic audit and discovered that Amy had been stealing money. When questioned, she admitted to embezzling funds and making up the robbery story to cover her thieving. The police hadn't even bothered to inform Abel that they no longer suspected him of the crime.

Even though there's lots of strange information in Amy's 911 call – that she doesn't know what kind of weapon the robber had but then says it was a handgun, and the confusion in her description of the robber, reeling off different ethnicities after claiming the robber had a mask on – what I want to draw your attention to is how she uses lots of 'um's when answering the operator's questions. Those 'um's and 'er's that occur when we all speak are called filled pauses. Generally, we all have a negative perception of those who use many of these filled pauses and assume that they are reticent, unsure, unknowledgeable, guessing or just plain making something up.

Filled pauses occur all the time in our speech, although normally we do not notice them.[35] This is because we 'filter' out these sounds, deeming them unimportant. When we listen to someone speak, there are many things that we attend to: individual words, the grammatical structure of the sentences, pronunciation, paralinguistic cues, the organisation of the narrative, the content, body language, gestures and so on. Our attention only has limited capacity, which means that some of it will remain unnoticed, or filtered out.

Filled pauses are more likely to occur at the beginning of an utterance or phrase, like in Amy's answers. One reason why they occur is that they are produced when there is a delay to the speaker's speech plan. This delay can be caused by a greater cognitive load on the speaker; for example, if the topic is unfamiliar, then the speaker has to think more.[36] When filled pauses occur within an utterance (like in the middle of a sentence), it could also be due to a higher cognitive load caused by the speaker making a choice from a selection of words. When we lie, we have to be careful about what we say, so we can expect a delay and more 'um's and 'er's to fill that space.

The use of filled pauses can convey other information too, such as a speaker's confidence in what they are saying. Less confident speech and being self-conscious gives rise to sentence-initial filled pauses;[37] however, this is not indicative of overall anxiety (unlike other paraverbal indicators). Filled pauses also occur when a speaker wants to 'keep the floor': when they have not yet finished speaking and are signalling that they want to carry on.[38]

As with any form of scientific investigation, sometimes research into deception cues in language produces conflicting results. A few studies find that the filled pause 'um' shows a reduced indication of deception.[39] This research uses a generally accepted research paradigm or method of conducting research for eliciting lies experimentally. Thirty-two undergraduate student participants were given a social issues questionnaire and told they would be asked in an interview to lie or tell the truth about their opinion on some of the social issues. When they lied, they were told to try to convince the interviewer that they held the opposite opinion to their beliefs. The interviews were recorded and the results were analysed for the occurrence of frequency of 'um' in both truth-telling and lying instances. The results from this study concluded that there were more instances of 'um' in the truth-telling answers. This may be because other research has found that 'um' is used by speakers when they are trying to decide what to say,[40] which we would expect in both truth-tellers and liars.

However, some liars may be able to strategically control their use of 'um's and 'er's, particularly those who are good at avoiding certain language behaviours that they may consider as indicating deception.[41] This could explain why there are fewer filled pauses in the speech of liars in studies addressing this verbal behaviour. In order to avoid appearing like they are floundering or thinking about their answers – as the hearer might start to mistrust them – someone who is lying may try to reduce their use of filled pauses.[42] When filled pauses do occur, it could be when a liar is taken off guard or if they are telling a difficult lie.[43] Similarly, filled pauses can occur when a liar is carefully selecting their words, and other studies have indeed found an increase in filled pauses when speakers are having to really concentrate on what they are saying,[44] such as when they are being deceptive. For example, increases in filled pauses are found in deceptive speech from a more rigorous study which uses a larger participant cohort. These participants watched a real-life scenario of a video of the theft of a bag by a patient or visitor in a setting which was more relevant to them (as nurses in a hospital). The participants were interviewed twice about the video, once where they had to tell the truth and a second time where they had to lie about the theft. The interviews were recorded and the results analysed to find, aside from other language-related cues to deception, that filled pauses like 'um' did occur more frequently in the speech of the participants when they were lying.[45]

What this means is that we should listen out for 'um's as they can be an indicator of complex lying, when a liar is having to really think about what it is they should say (decision-making lies) or when a liar is taken by surprise. Practised liars may avoid appearing deceptive by controlling the occurrence of filled pauses in their speech. But that does not mean they won't be caught out by another type of pause and that's the unfilled kind.

## The sound of silence

St Margaret's Church in Barking, East London, is built on a site that dates back to the thirteenth century. With its distinctive stone clock tower, this somewhat typical English church is circled by flintstone walls, enclosing an old graveyard. In the summer of 2014, Barbara was walking her eleven-year-old border collie dog Max, as she did regularly, through the church's graveyard. It was a lovely quiet walk; the trees were in full leaf, the sun was shining, and the church bells chimed the hour.

Ambling past one of the graveyard's walls, Barbara spotted a young man wearing dark glasses. He was sitting down with his legs stretched out, leaning with his back against the wall. With his sunglasses askew, he looked to Barbara as if he was sleeping off a heavy night of drinking. But when her dog went running up to the young man and he failed to rouse, Barbara became concerned: 'I thought he hasn't moved, he hasn't flinched. It doesn't look right.' She decided to approach the young man, clapping her hands in front of his face and shouting: 'Woo hoo,' to try to wake him. But the young man remained still. Growing more concerned now, Barbara gently touched his hand and immediately recoiled. He was ice cold. Barbara called the police.

The coroner later concluded that the young man, only

in his twenties, had died from an overdose of recreational drugs. Barbara tried to put this distressing event out of her mind and carried on with her daily life.

A month to the day after discovering the young man, Barbara was out again walking Max in the grounds of St Margaret's Church. It was now September, the leaves were starting to turn brown on the trees, there was a slight chill in the air and the days were shortening. Just as Barbara was nearing the same sad place where she had found the young man, she froze to a standstill. There, propped up against the exact same spot, was another young man. Barbara thought to herself: 'Please God no, please not another one. Please let it be a boy who's drunk.' Tentatively, Barbara approached him and noticed he was about the same age as the first young man. She bent down and gently touched the skin on his outstretched leg. He too was ice cold.

The police questioned Barbara. After all, it was strange that she should find two young men, both dead in the exact same spot. They needed to ensure that she had nothing to do with these deaths. After discovering what looked to be a suicide note in this young man's hand, they concluded that he had died by his own hand, blaming himself for the death of his apparent friend – the other young man.

Sadly, more young men were later found in the graveyard. Stephen Port was a local male escort who was found to have drugged and murdered these young men he had met through online dating sites. After plying them with fatal amounts of recreational drugs, Port dumped their bodies around St Margaret's Churchyard. It took the police many months to link the murders together and to uncover Stephen Port's role in these young men's terrible deaths.

When interviewed by the police after they found incriminating evidence in his internet browsing history, Port's reply is quite revealing:

> **Police:** 'You're specifically searching for videos of porn to do with people who are either asleep or have been drugged and are being raped. You've typed in the word "rape" haven't you?'
>
> **Port:** '[three-second delay] Er [three-second unfilled pause] yeah that's just [three-second unfilled pause] that's just searching for random videos nothing specific.'[46]

Port uses unfilled pauses, which are either grammatical pauses that occur between sentences, clauses or phrases, or ungrammatical pauses that occur at inappropriate places where they should not really occur,[47] such as before a function word like 'that' (function words express grammatical relationships between other words in a sentence). Both these types of pauses are different from the period of silence which is sometimes found when an individual starts to speak, which is called response latency (we will look at this a bit later). Research into pauses suggests that unfilled pauses are a far more reliable indicator of speaker anxiety than filled pauses.[48]

These periods of silence can also reveal an individual's personality characteristics. Individuals who are reserved, cold, suspicious, insecure and tense tend to produce longer pauses in their speech.[49] A very interesting revelation is that longer unfilled pauses are also more prevalent in the speech of liars.[50] This could be because lying is anxiety-inducing, or because, as mentioned, some liars will actively avoid using 'um's and 'er's, and these longer pauses give them the time they need to monitor their word choices.[51]

Unfilled pauses can be a real giveaway. When the American financier Bernie Madoff, who defrauded thousands of people, tries to defend himself to a New York magazine reporter, he says:

'Did people lose um [pause] profits that they thought they'd made? Yeah.'[52]

We can hear that he uses an unfilled pause straight after filled pauses. Pauses like these indicate that liars are at a semantic planning point:[53] searching for a suitable word or unit of speech that does not reveal that they are lying, or saying something that could incriminate them, or that would jeopardise something they have said already. Madoff carefully selects the word 'profits' at this point rather than the more truthful 'life savings'.

The number and length of unfilled pauses can increase as the task of planning gets more difficult, especially if speakers are asked unanticipated questions. Those poor liars that need to prepare what they say will also struggle with another type of unfilled pause, and that's the one right before they say anything.

## Take your time

There's a certain long unfilled pause that is a good paraverbal indicator of lying, and this is the one right before you start speaking. This is called response latency. Response latency is the length of time between the end of one speaker's turn or question, and the point at which the second speaker's response or answer begins.[54] We inherently know that we take turns when we converse with each other (which is why it is rude to speak when someone else has not finished), and this turn-taking is universally exceedingly quick, usually between 100 and 300 milliseconds.[55] This means that we are able to predict when a speaker's turn is coming to the end, and we prepare to take our turn in advance.[56]

Measuring the response time of an individual's answer is a powerful tool in detecting lies.[57] We take longer in our response times if we need to plan or construct a careful answer.[58] There is only one truth but many possible lie options, and choosing which lie to tell impacts the response time of replies.[59] As there is an increase in cognitive load, we expect that liars will need more processing and planning time – although if they have had enough time to rehearse or prepare their lies, then there can be no discernible difference in response times between true or false responses.[60] This means that measuring response times is helpful if liars have not had time to prepare their lies.

With the serial killer Stephen Port, we notice that not only does he leave unfilled pauses in his answers to the police's questions, but he also takes his time in answering:

> **Police:** 'You're searching for boy drugged rape etc, why's that?'
>
> **Port:** '[three-second delay] Um [three-second delay] well just generally looking for general porn um.'[61]

In his answer to the police's questions, this murderer has three-second response latencies. His delays are followed by a filled pause before he starts to give an explanation. These delays indicate that he is searching for a valid or acceptable answer, as he knows this evidence is highly incriminating.

Response times also vary due to differences in the type of question. For example, if a question just requires a 'yes' or 'no' answer like: 'Did you pack this bag yourself?' then there is less variation between a truth-teller and a liar's response time.⁶² But if an open-ended question or a content question is asked, and if the liar has not rehearsed the answer, then the variance in response time is more notable.⁶³ It is obvious that responding 'yes' or 'no' to a closed question is quicker than responding to one that requires added complexity, regardless of whether you are doing so truthfully. It can also take longer to reply truthfully to open-ended questions as well. For example, if you were asked about where you were last Thursday evening, it might take you some time to remember.

In measuring response times as an indicator of deception, it is most important to consider whether the type of question asked is something the other person would anticipate. In other words, the interactive environment (question-and-answer pairs, and whether they are anticipated) needs careful consideration. Response latency is a cognitive-load cue to deception, so the more effort the speaker has to make in their response, the more likely they will take their time in answering.

A tricky and unexpected question was put to a man who murdered his pregnant girlfriend. During a televised appeal, a journalist asks if he can remember his last conversation with his girlfriend before she went missing. This is his reply:

**Tessier:** '[eleven-second delay] I don't know where she is that's all, I don't know, like I don't [three-second unfilled pause] we're all doing everything we can to try to find her and [three-second unfilled pause] I just pray that [three-second unfilled pause] I pray that she's safe [unfilled pause] that she comes back [unfilled pause] that's all I care about right now.'⁶⁴

There is a whopping eleven-second response latency in this liar's answer. He probably did have a last conversation with his girlfriend, but he really does not want to reveal what it was. Instead, he is delayed so much in his response that he goes on to answer a completely different question. His speech throughout is full of unfilled pauses. He is so lost for words, it's a wonder he even bothers trying to lie.

Not that long ago, my friend was looking for a place to live. She had found somewhere that appeared perfect and invited me to go with her to view the property. The landlord was showing us around, saying what a great place it was. He was chatty and seemed very open, informing us of all the mod cons the flat came with, and the amenities in the local area. However, when my friend asked him what the neighbours were like, he paused for a bit too long before replying: '[three-second pause] They seem fine.' His response latency indicated to me that he was being deceptive, and that these neighbours were probably not 'fine'. I told my friend, who decided to investigate my suspicion and returned a few days later to speak to the tenants. The tenants told her that the neighbours were not fine at all: they were awful – loud music, arguments, doors banging all night – which is why the present tenants were moving out, despite having told the landlord many times. My friend decided to find somewhere else to live.

## My mistake

Stumbling over words, self-corrections and starting to say something and then stopping (false starts) are all types of speech errors and can signal deceptive speech[65] as these speech errors occur commonly with heightened anxiety.[66] These speech errors also usually occur when a speaker is taken off guard by a question, especially one that they have not prepared or planned to answer. Rather than admitting that they don't know the answer to a question, they might stumble over their words to mask their lack of knowledge. And when these speech errors occur, they reduce the comprehensibility of what someone is saying and it appears muddled. That's what happened to Barack Obama at a talk he gave in Bristol, Virginia, when he spoke about healthcare reforms:

> 'What they'll say is, it'll cost too much money. But you know what? It will cost about, it it it will cost about the same as what we would spend [three-second pause] it over the course of ten years it will cost what it costs us it will huh [pause] all right OK

we're going to. It will cost about the same as it would cost [pause] for about.'[67]

So Obama didn't know what the reform would cost and tried to make out that he did, and stumbled over his words. We are all very attuned to this type of speech, and as soon as a speaker stumbles, self-corrects, or makes false starts and keeps stopping, it raises our suspicion of the veracity of what they are saying.

Just the other day while travelling out of London on a train, I heard an exchange between a ticket inspector and a passenger that showed stumbles and self-corrections that gave his lie-invention away. The passenger was a young man travelling without a ticket, claiming the machine was broken at the station. The inspector needed to take some details and asked the young man for his name and address. He answered: 'It's [pause] my address is, I live um at . . .' With an unplanned liar like this we would be right to be suspicious, which the inspector was. We should listen out for false starts, stumbling over words or changing sentences mid-way, as these can all be indications that a speaker is lying, just like this young man who received a fine for his poorly prepared lie.

In a very recent and highly publicised court trial, an ex-couple were suing each other for defamation with allegations of domestic abuse on both sides. Have a look at this transcript from the trial:

## HOW TO DETECT LIES IN VOCAL CUES

**Lawyer:** 'And how did you sustain that bruise?'

**Defendant:** 'I was [pause] I had thrown a [pause] well [name] slapped me.'

There are some false starts in the defendant's response which might indicate fabrication, but I'll leave you to decide for yourself.

Deceptive language is not only about the things that we say, but how we say them. Paying close attention to the way in which words are spoken can be one of the most powerful methods for determining if someone is being truthful. Generally, we filter out a speaker's disfluency of false starts – however, when we transcribe exactly what a speaker is saying, we are able to see these mistakes more clearly. This shows us how we process language differently when we read as opposed to hear it. Think about novels with dialogue, for instance – do you ever read pauses (filled or unfilled), false starts, stumbles or mid-way sentence changes? Not usually. This is because it is hard to process them in writing, so authors generally don't include them, but this is not the way that people really talk. It is fairly normal for us to start saying something and then change the direction, but if we hear it often or for longer durations when someone is being asked questions about something suspicious, that should grab our attention.

I've shown you now the most important parts of

speech to watch out for to help you uncover lies. But that's only one part of your role as a linguistic lie detector. You also have to learn how to be a better listener, and how to uncover lies with your own strategic use of language. That's where we will go next.

CHAPTER 4

# Prepare: How to get ready for linguistic lie detection

Now that you are familiar with the many different ways that language can indicate a speaker may be lying, we are going to turn to your role in any conversation or interview with a potential liar. Because the language we all use is guided by our self-presentation, as speakers we pay attention to the listener and how the listener is interpreting and reacting to what we are saying moment by moment. It's important to consider your role as the listener. Lies are told *to* someone – they are not told to an empty room. This someone is called the conversational partner. The role of the conversational partner is hugely important, and they are the one who ultimately decides if the speaker's lie is successful or not. A lie has to be believed for it to have worked. So, now we are going to look at your role as the conversational partner, and how you can adapt your thinking, the things you say and the questions you ask in order to uncover the truth.[1]

## Listen carefully

The first step is that you need to listen carefully to what other people say. Sounds simple, right?[2] Yet most of us do not actively listen when other people are speaking; we could be distracted, occupied, uninterested or anticipating our turn, composing what we want to say in our heads.[3] This is all due to a lack of focus or attention. Try to concentrate, pay attention and turn off your own inner voice, stop preparing what you want to say and instead focus very closely on the other person, how they are speaking and the words and grammar they are using. Try to keep your mind or your thoughts silent – and just listen.

The second step is to consider whether the speaker has had the time or the opportunity to prepare their lies. This is because if lies have been prepared then the liar is accessing a script or a familiar story to base their lies on, and it may make your job as a lie detector a bit harder. For example, that deceiving partner who spent the night conducting an illicit affair but works from a script when they tell you they were at a friend's: they may be using their memory of the familiar house as the backstory for their lie and so have reduced their cognitive effort. It does not mean that these scripted or planned lies don't contain any cues to the deceit, as they may still be shorter and less detailed.[4] But you must consider whether the lies you are listening to are spontaneous or scripted.

## HOW TO GET READY FOR LINGUISTIC LIE DETECTION

The third step is that you need to remember that language adapts and evolves to each different communicative context. Language is a dynamic process often modified and shaped to fit the social setting in which we speak. Think for a moment about how you alter your language use from when you talk with friends and family to how you speak with unfamiliar others – strangers or authority figures. We all naturally adjust our language in response to who we are talking to and the social setting that we are in.

It is no different with liars.

If we want to analyse a speaker's language use for indications of lying, it means that we must not only consider the things they say – the *content*, but we must be aware of the *context* in which they say them. What is the social setting? Is it formal or informal? Is there a power imbalance? The speaker could be in an interview setting, they may be speaking with someone in authority or a professional. If so, then a speaker who is lying does not only have to consciously and constantly adapt their responses to ensure they do not incriminate themselves, but they also must adhere to the interactional setting of question-and-answer turn-taking. Their answers then may be limited.

Who are they speaking with? Is it a stranger, someone close, work colleagues? The relationship between the conversational partners is important, as individuals are more likely to lie to strangers than friends,[5] and people lie less frequently to those they are close to,[6] and if they do lie then they are more likely to feel discomfort. What is the physical setting? Is the speaker in familiar or unfamiliar surroundings? We should also consider what are the goals and intentions behind the speaker's utterance – what do they want? For example, if it is a business negotiation, then there is a high incentive in which to mislead others.[7] If a speaker's goal is to secure a job, then during their interview, their propensity to lie through exaggeration is increased.[8] Are they making a promise, a request or warning? Are they putting their side of an event forward? Are they trying to convince the listener of something?[9]

The content of what a speaker says should always be assessed with an awareness of the context in which they say it. Different cues to deception are used depending upon the setting. Considering your role as the conversational partner and what you say in the sequence of the communication is also vital. We will look at the role of the conversational partner a bit later, but first there are a few other things you must keep in mind in linguistic lie detection.

## The truth hurts – ignore psychological lies

Let's start with those questions that we ask each other every day that will nearly always be answered with a lie. These specific untruths are called psychological or

## HOW TO GET READY FOR LINGUISTIC LIE DETECTION

prosocial lies – but we also call them 'white lies' – which are told to reduce harm, avoid hurt feelings and lessen tension. They allow us to hide what we really think and we are all guilty of telling these lies. We tell them to avoid conflict or awkwardness; they protect us and others from the truth. Sometimes, it's just easier to lie than to be honest. These are those harmless lies that are usually told as face-saving untruths – to avoid embarrassing yourself or someone else. You've probably told a few of these. Perhaps, rather than admit you didn't want to speak to someone, you've made out that your phone ran out of battery, or you were late in submitting a piece of work so you claim that your computer has bad Wi-Fi/internet connection. Maybe, like many of my students did when I was teaching online throughout Covid, you've fibbed that your laptop camera has stopped working when you're in an online lesson or meeting. Perhaps you've called in sick to work with food poisoning when it was really that you had a bit too much to drink the night before. Or told your doctor that you only drink a third of what you really drink, and that you exercise regularly. You've almost certainly told someone they look well when they clearly don't.

This type of lying is a common feature of everyday communication. It mostly has little importance in daily life, and we don't judge each other that badly when we hear these white lies as there is an unspoken code that they are socially acceptable. If you hear one of these psychological lies, then you usually play along. You want to 'save face': go along with the deception to avoid shaming or damaging the other person's reputation or feelings. Sometimes, it's best not to call out a liar when doing so would damage their sense of self and there's not much to be gained from the truth. We all lie like this, although on average women tell more psychological lies than men.[10]

There are also altruistic lies. These are distinct from psychological lies as they are 'false statements that are costly for the liar and are made with the intention of misleading and benefitting a target'.[11] For instance, a doctor may choose to lie to a dying patient about the prognosis in order to give them comfort in the final weeks of their life.[12] These altruistic lies may benefit the patient by soothing their remaining days, but could be costly for the doctor as doing so might violate ethical standards or invite litigation. Psychological or prosocial lying is not always motivated by selfish intentions, and sometimes it is the intent behind lies which matters more than the truth.[13]

## It's not always emotional

It is crucial to keep in mind that people display emotions in varying ways. When recalling a negative or upsetting experience, some people may cry or show signs of distress and others may display no real discernible emotion. Individual differences in personality mean that people exhibit

## HOW TO GET READY FOR LINGUISTIC LIE DETECTION

different emotional responses to similar events. However, it is a common misconception that people who do not show any real emotional response are in some way being deceitful, and that a truthful individual is more likely to be emotional.[14]

When my brother and I were young teenagers, he thought it would be funny to tell our mother that he'd seen me smoking. He even went as far as planting a lighter in my school bag, which he miraculously found and presented as evidence. When our mother confronted me, he was standing behind her grinning, revelling in the fact that his lie had been believed. I shouted my denial, bellowed that he was setting me up, and berated my mother for falling for his lies. When she believed my brother, I demanded to know why she thought I was lying. She explained that because I had got so worked up and angry, I must be lying – attack is the best form of defence, after all. My brother took delight for many years in the success of his lie.

The truth is we are all different, and therefore we all display varying emotional reactions to different situations. Whether someone is emotional or not isn't a good sign that they are being deceitful, as it's more likely to be a product of their individual approach. Emotional responses can be manipulated, like those crocodile tears or fake crying, or even pretend outrage, so make sure you are not relying on emotional cues to differentiate between liars and truth-tellers as it is rarely reliable.

## Pay attention

Being human means that we all have an innate tendency to trust rather than to distrust what we are told.[15] This leads us to accept most information as truthful in the first instance – innocent until proven guilty. This is known as truth bias.[16] It is an instance of something called 'heuristic processing', which is effectively a cognitive or mental shortcut to make judgements or solve problems quickly and with the least effort. This means that we all ignore some information, consciously or unconsciously, to favour the truth. Our innateness to trust is also integral to humans as a social animal. Much of our knowledge about the world comes from what others tell us (our parents, teachers, friends, colleagues), so from a young age, we are conditioned to have implicit trust in the information that others share with us. It is our default setting. Without this, our relationships would be strained, full of untold problems and discord, and ultimately communication and our relationships with each other would fail.

Our natural tendency to trust does make us susceptible to believing lies, particularly if we are not actively listening. We are not only hard-wired to trust information we hear, but we also have a limited attention capacity. This means that when our attention is oriented towards one thing, it reduces how attentive we are able to be towards other things. In essence, we do not have enough attention to respond to all the potentially relevant information in our environment.[17] A well-known experiment showed how this limited attention capacity works. During a basketball game, spectators were instructed to count the number of basketball passes made by a group of players. While focusing on counting these passes, the spectators failed to notice that a man dressed as a gorilla walked through the basketball game.[18] Our inability to notice quite obvious things because our attention is elsewhere, explains why we may fail to notice deception.[19]

An example of this is the question dodge; when 'speakers answer a question that is similar enough to the question asked, listeners may fail to notice that the answer offered is, in fact, irrelevant'.[20] Here's an instance from Anthony Weiner again, that US Congressman whose lies became known as Weinergate. He is being further interviewed about allegations of 'sexting':

> **Interviewer:** 'Have you ever taken a picture like this [shows photo from text message of a man's genitals] of yourself?'
>
> **Weiner:** 'I can tell you this, there are, I have photographs, I don't know what photographs are out there in the world of me, I don't know what's been manipulated and doctored, um and we are gonna try and find out what happened.'[21]

Weiner didn't answer the question, he dodged it by speaking about photographs, which kept his answer within the boundaries of similarity to the question asked. He was being deceitful though, as he had sent images of his genitalia quite a few times.

Question dodging or evasion is a technique often used by politicians. Margaret Thatcher, the former UK Prime Minister, famously admitted: 'You don't tell deliberate lies, but sometimes you have to be evasive.' Being evasive or dodging a question is an effective strategy for deceiving a listener, as we mostly don't realise it's happening because we are attending to other goals, usually automatic ones. For instance, when we meet someone new, the automatic social goal of evaluating that person reduces our attention to what they are saying. We pay more attention to things like: Do we like this new person? Do they seem nice?[22] As the social goal of forming an impression of others is automatic and a default, it makes us as listeners susceptible to being deceived.[23] Along with our ingrained truth-bias, it means that we generally don't take a critical approach to what we are hearing. Our interaction with others demands a great deal of our attention, which ultimately leads to us being vulnerable to deception.

Understanding that we have a limited attention capacity does not mean that we are gullible to all forms of deception. But it does mean that we have to place extra focus in listening, particularly when the answers are dissimilar to the question asked.

## Gaslighting

Our innate tendency to trust information also leaves us vulnerable to others manipulating our perception of reality. This manipulation tactic is known as 'gaslighting'. It takes its name from Patrick Hamilton's 1938 play and the 1944 film *Gaslight*, about a husband who gradually tries to convince his wife that she is going mad. One of the ways that he does this is by making the gaslights in their home flicker, and when the wife points this out, he insists she must be imagining it. As he constantly denies his wife's claims, she starts to question her own perceptions, memories and observations, and begins to believe she must be going insane. Recently there has been a resurgence of interest in gaslighting, with the term used to describe a variety of manipulative behaviours.[24]

Gaslighting is a common technique of abusers[25] and those with certain personality disorders, such as sociopaths and narcissists. Used primarily as a power tactic, gaslighting can take many forms, always with the aim of making the victim question their sanity. Its main form is lying and strong denial. No amount of reasoning or proof will get the gaslighter to accept they are lying, and they will steadfastly deny that they did or said something. If you're the conversational partner to someone who is attempting to gaslight you, you might start to question your own reality and lose trust in yourself. This makes it harder to spot further deceptions down the line. If you get to the point where you are questioning what you know to be true, be alert to the fact that you may be dealing with a gaslighter.

Thankfully, there are a few things you can start doing to spot when you are being lied to: firstly, don't assume that everything you hear is true, and secondly, pay close attention to what other people say. Once you learn to do this, you can then focus on specific areas that can signal if someone is being deceptive, although you'll also have to learn some self-reflection as we all make judgements about other people which can lead us to incorrect assumptions.

## Don't judge the accent

Between 1989 and 1996, there were multiple indecent assaults on young girls in the county of Surrey, UK. These girls in their early teens were assaulted while walking in local beauty spots. The attacker, sometimes armed with a knife, evaded capture for over seventeen years. An extensive police investigation and many appeals on national television led nowhere. Detectives just couldn't find this deviant and dangerous assailant, even though they had a description of him. They were searching for a scruffy man who looked like a tramp and wore sunglasses.

Not only was this attacker's unkempt appearance quite distinctive in this very affluent area of expensive houses and well-dressed professionals, but so was his voice. He spoke with a cockney accent which was a sure indication that he was most likely working class and from the London area. Investigators believed that this sexual predator's voice and attire stood out enough in the somewhat well-heeled area of Surrey for someone to know or identify him. But no one did. After the last known attack in 1996, the case was left open, remaining unsolved until an unconnected incident happened many years later.

Anthony was a middle-aged architect who had a well-paid job working for a south London local authority. A married father of two, Anthony was brought up in Kent, where he received a private education. Well respected in his job and local community, Anthony was considered by those who knew him as a gentle-natured, well-spoken and respectable man – a Mr Nice Guy.

In February 2005, Anthony's elderly father had broken his leg. As he needed support, Anthony's sister decided that their father should move closer to her once he was discharged from hospital. While she was making these arrangements, she looked over their father's bank accounts. She didn't like what she saw: there seemed to be money missing. Assuming that Anthony must be responsible, she called the police who arrested him on suspicion of theft. As any individual who is arrested in the UK automatically has their DNA taken, Anthony had a DNA swab taken at the station before the theft allegation was dropped.

Not long afterwards, Anthony was arrested again. This time for indecent assault. His DNA sample had been matched by the Metropolitan Police's cold case review team to samples taken from the sexual assaults of the Surrey schoolgirls. This impeccably presented, well-spoken architect was the attacker. He had disguised his true self and voice by adopting the persona of someone who is the opposite to what he was: a cockney vagrant.

His ruse had worked for many years, as the police were looking for someone who didn't match Anthony's description at all. But the DNA evidence meant the courts could convict him of these awful attacks, all committed within a radius of twenty miles of his home in Surrey. This cockney impersonator was imprisoned for thirteen years. Knowing that he had an educated, well-spoken accent, Anthony falsified his voice to make it harder for anyone to match him to the crimes.

Anthony's fake accent fooled the police for many years, although a speaker's accent can also fool us as we make judgements about an individual's honesty based upon their accent. We can think of 'accent' as the way you sound when you speak. Our accents can be formed through our individual, regional, social or national backgrounds. You may think that you don't have an accent,

## HOW TO GET READY FOR LINGUISTIC LIE DETECTION

although this is not true as everyone speaks with an accent. It is just that you are more likely to hear accents in speakers who do not come from your background.

Our ability to detect accents is formed when we are babies; from five months old, we can identify accent variation in English dialects.[26] We can also rapidly spot that a speaker is non-native from their accent in as little as thirty milliseconds.[27] We all make judgements of speakers based upon their accent, whether they have native accents or not. Within the UK, there are roughly forty different regional accents, whereas in the US, which is over forty times bigger than the UK, there are probably only about twenty different regional accents – the reasons for this are historic and to do with migration and invasion patterns. You might already know intuitively that speakers of any language prefer native accents to non-native ones.[28] And we don't just prefer native accents, we are actually less likely to believe non-native speakers.[29] Non-native speakers appear to us less credible[30] and trustworthy and, worryingly, they are more likely to receive harsher sentences in legal settings.[31]

Your perception and judgement of accents can be influenced by your own linguistic background. The less familiar with or exposed to different accents you are, the more likely you are to have a harsher or more negative perception of accented speakers.[32] For example, teachers who work with non-native speakers are less likely to think of these speakers negatively than those people who do not encounter non-native speakers much in their day-to-day lives. So why is our assessment of speakers' truth-telling or deception influenced by their accent?[33]

The reason for this could be because non-native speech is harder to understand than native speech, which results in listeners having a processing difficulty, which causes non-native speakers to sound less credible.[34] Perceptual fluency – the ease with which we perceive language – is found to increase our believability in what someone says.[35] It could also be due to the truth-bias, which appears to lean us more favourably towards native-language speakers as opposed to non-native-language speakers.[36] It could be the case of 'stranger danger': we are biased towards our kith and kin; outsiders naturally raise our suspicions.

However, judging non-native-language speakers' accounts as less trustworthy could be to do with changes in language use that appear in English as indications of deception. For instance, in English, an account of an event has a templatic structure – the introduction is usually short and orienting, such as scene-setting, which then moves to the main events, told in chronological order. If there is a departure from this structure, or events are skipped over, or speakers detail irrelevant information and not crucial information, or there is a lack of cohesion, or a decrease in fact-telling etc., then it indicates deception on the part of the speaker. But non-native-language speakers are more likely to deviate from

## HOW TO GET READY FOR LINGUISTIC LIE DETECTION

this type of account description or storytelling, and it is not because they are being deceptive. It is because other cultures have different ways of expressing a narrative, such as an account of an event, an experience or relating a story. Storytelling in other cultures can be interactive, where there is audience (or listener) participation, and can involve more circuitous routes to the point of the story.[37] Therefore, if the coherence of the non-native-language speaker's narrative appears odd to the native English speaker, then the non-native speaker is more likely to be assumed to be lying.

Similarly, there are many aspects of speech that non-native speakers exhibit which correspond with deceptive verbal cues: easily accessed simple and concrete words, less abstract ones and an increased use of repetitions and hesitations.[38] So you will have to remember not to judge a speaker's accent when assessing veracity, and keep an ear out for any correspondences a second-language speaker may have with certain deceptive cues.

## Don't trust the good guy

You might want to treat with suspicion those who use their character as a reason why they could not possibly be responsible for doing something. If someone is asked if they are having an affair, and their reply is that they are happily married, it might be an instance of a character lie. Or perhaps an employee who is questioned about stolen money may respond that they have worked for their employer for many years. These types of responses are used by individuals as a way of denying the claim put forward by appealing to their own good character. These types of replies are implying that: 'It is impossible I could have committed the offence because I do not possess the characteristics which are needed to commit the offence or transgression.'

In 2007, the *National Enquirer* ran a story alleging that John Edwards, a US Senator, was having an affair with a young female aide. When asked by a reporter for his reaction to the allegation, this is what Edwards responded:

> 'The story's false, it's completely untrue, ridiculous er I've been in love with the same woman for thirty-plus years and as anybody that's been around us knows she's an extraordinary human being er warm, loving, beautiful, sexy er and as good a person as I've ever known so the story's just false.'[39]

It was later revealed that not only was Edwards indeed having an affair, but he had also fathered a child with his mistress. Just because an individual has been in love with the same woman for years or is happily married does not mean they are incapable of having an affair, and an employee may have worked for a long time for

## HOW TO GET READY FOR LINGUISTIC LIE DETECTION

an employer but it does not mean that they are incapable of stealing money. In one particularly gruesome murder trial, the defendant – who was later convicted of having met another man through a dating app, murdered him, dismembered his body and partially dissolved it in acid – claimed that the death of the victim was accidental and caused by a bondage game gone wrong. He could not have murdered the victim as he was, he said, 'just a nice guy'.[40]

When individuals refer to their good character or positive past actions, we should be wary that they could be trying to influence us, informing us of their positive character traits, rather than answering the question we are asking of them or addressing the accusation directly.

But what about if someone does look like a good guy? Should we trust what they say? The answer is definitely no. That's because we are all susceptible to something called 'demeanour bias'. This is a trait judgement we all have of each other that you also need to watch out for. We tend to attribute trustworthiness based upon appearance, manner or conduct. What this means is we assume that what a person says must be trustworthy if they look trustworthy. For example, if they look to us as though they possess positive traits such as appearing likeable, honest, kind, gentle, happy, confident etc., or if they are attractive or pleasant looking. We are influenced by how a person looks as to whether we think they are a liar or not.[41] Less attractive individuals or those who don't appear to possess positive traits are less likely to be trusted. This type of demeanour bias of facial features can affect applicant success in interviews,[42] election outcomes[43] and the sentencing of defendants in court. Attractive defendants are more likely to be found not guilty, or to receive shorter sentences, and are considered less dangerous than those defendants who are unattractive.[44] What we look like therefore interacts with how honest we appear to others and how trustworthy they think we are. You'll need to learn not to trust your eyes in this regard, and sometimes your ears as well when it comes to being biased with accents, if you want to be better at deception detection.

## The truth can be a lie

Usually, lies either leave information out (omission) or include information (commission) that is not true. There is a third surprising way that lies can be told – by using the truth to lie. This type of lying uses a truthful statement to create a lie or false impression. The story of the Captain and his Mate is a good example of this:

A captain and his mate have a long-term quarrel. The mate drinks more rum than is good for him, and the captain is determined not to tolerate his behaviour any longer. One time, when the mate is drunk, the captain

## HOW TO GET READY FOR LINGUISTIC LIE DETECTION

writes in the ship logbook: '*Today, 11th October, the mate is drunk.*' When the mate reads this entry during his next watch, he initially gets angry, and then, after a short moment of reflection, he writes in the logbook: '*Today, 14th October, the captain is not drunk.*'[45]

It is true that the captain is not drunk, but the mate is implying that the captain is drunk every other day and that this day is an exception, so worth writing about. Lying is not only making an intentionally false statement,[46] it is also making true statements with the aim to deceive. This reminds me of a line from William Blake's poem 'Auguries of Innocence': 'A truth that's told with bad intent, beats all the lies you can invent.'[47]

Politicians and salespeople are usually quite good at this, as was a colleague of mine from many years ago. Before starting university, I worked in a small customer complaints team where my main role was to deal with irate holidaymakers who rang up with problems – usually delivered with plenty of swearing and abuse. The complaints ranged from there not being enough men in the resort, to finding faeces floating in the hotel pool. Even though the job was stressful, I enjoyed it as I also got to observe a colleague (we'll call her Rose) who was brilliant at lying by telling the truth.

Our manager was a real micromanager, who was constantly checking where we were. If someone left their desk, he would march over and ask us all where they were. Instead of replying that the person in question was on their tea/lunch/toilet break (which they were), Rose would say things like: 'He left for work yesterday at the right time.' Once, the manager asked if a particular colleague had made a personal call, and Rose responded: 'I did not hear them make a work call.' I was quite fascinated by the way that Rose used the truth to lie, and how she effectively used language to deceive. She could get her colleagues into trouble, yet insist that she had not lied.

We need to watch out for this way of using language to hide the truth, especially as it is commonly used by negotiators and salespersons.[48] Focus on keeping alert to whether answers specifically match your question. If they do not, ask the same question again. Listen closely to answers that leave out or change certain keywords. If you ask a seller if there have been any problems with an item, the reply you should expect is either: 'No, there's not been any problem with it,' or: 'Yes, there has been a problem with the item.' Any other form of reply should ring alarm bells.

You also need to be aware when you are making a connection yourself, rather than receiving an exact answer. Any additional words require consideration. For instance, in asking about a second-hand washing machine, you might ask: 'Does it work OK?' to which the seller might reply: 'It seems to work OK.' But you didn't ask if it *seems* to work, you asked if it *does* work. Buyer beware!

HOW TO GET READY FOR LINGUISTIC LIE DETECTION

## The same is not the truth

Sometimes two or more people tell us the same thing and this makes us think that it must be the truth. Well, not always. It could be an instance of collusion. Primarily, people who are colluding will work out their story together; they decide on the facts that they need to tell to appear consistent and avert any suspicion. They need to corroborate each other's stories.

But again, if you listen closely, their language can give them away. If multiple people's stories are *too* similar, it is possible that they have invented what they are saying and are 'sticking to the same story'. We do not remember events in the same way: we sense things that another person doesn't, and we notice different things. One person's interpretation of a situation will most often be different from someone else's. They may focus on different details; for example, one person may spot a car, whereas someone else may concentrate on the face of the driver. Add to that the fact that we often just remember things incorrectly. This is why eyewitness reliability has been extensively studied, and it is known that eyewitness testimonies are not always an exact recall of events.[49]

Regardless of any external stressors which affect recall ability (stress, anxiety, focus etc.), reconstructive memory is subject to personal interpretation and dependent on the way we make sense of the world: our learnt cultural norms and values.[50] As individuals, we interpret and focus on different things. This means that when the same event is recounted by different people, they will not always align or include the same details. We tend to remember our own actions better than other information. If there is total or near-total alignment in a group of people's stories, it can indicate that they have agreed their story beforehand, and that it is possibly a fabrication in parts.[51]

Listen carefully if a group of people are all telling the exact same story, as it can indicate that they have banded together to persuade you of a fabricated tale.

## I don't know

These three words make up the most spoken phrase in all the English language, both in the US and UK.[52] However, there are times when this phrase is not used as a declaration of a speaker's inability to supply information, but instead as a way to avoid answering a question by feigning a lack of knowledge. Perhaps the speaker wants to get out of making an assessment, introduce a disagreement, avoid an explicit disagreement, avoid committing, minimise impolite beliefs or mark uncertainty.[53] It is a multifunctional phrase which can convey deference or soften an assertion.[54] In all these uses, the phrase 'I don't know' arises when a speaker – for whatever reason – does not want to give an answer, even if they do, in fact, know.

## HOW TO GET READY FOR LINGUISTIC LIE DETECTION

You should pay attention to 'I don't know' when it is used as a direct response to a question with no additional information or suggestions. If we are telling the truth, we will often try to be helpful by supplying ideas or any other information we think may assist.[55] Let me give you an example of this, from when I had to interview one of my students who had submitted an essay that the university plagiarism software had detected as bought from an essay-mill (a business that supplies students with written essays). This is academic fraud and had to be investigated. When I interviewed this student and asked him why his essay matched the software identification, he replied: 'I don't know.' No offer of a suggestion as to why this could have happened was forthcoming, even after much prompting. If you think you are dealing with a liar who falsely claims they don't know, then ask them questions about what they *think* instead: What do they think happened? Who do they think did this? Why do they think this happened? You might just be able to catch them out. However, there is one group of people that commonly use 'I don't know' where no amount of questioning will elicit any further answers and that's teenagers. If you're the parent of a teenager, then you can be sure that you are regularly lied to. Out of all age groups, adolescents tell the most lies.[56] Teenagers lie more as they are testing out their independence by pushing boundaries and participating in risky behaviours. This means that teenagers will commonly lie to get out of trouble or to do something they are not allowed to do. When questioned, a typical response from a teenager is the much-used 'I don't know / Dunno' answer. It may be that no amount of questioning will elicit any other type of response from those uncommunicative teens.

## Keep it to yourself

Perhaps you do have evidence which supports your assumption that you are being lied to – if so, then you should delay disclosing it. Even if you think that the evidence will lead the liar to confess, if you approach with your evidence too soon, it shows someone that you are suspicious of them and they might close up. Also, if you disclose your evidence early on, they will know what you know and might change their story or give a plausible explanation instead – making your job harder. For instance, if I had been lying about smoking and had time to consider what I would say if I was caught, I could have given a credible story about why I had a lighter in my bag when my mother confronted me.

Similarly, it is pointless to ask accusatory questions, as they are usually answered with short denial responses by both truth-tellers and liars. When my mother accused me of smoking, of course I shouted: 'No, I'm not! It's a lie!' Very short denial responses come from a truth-teller as well as a liar. You need to ask questions that will give you the opportunity to draw out longer answers so you can analyse their language: the longer the answer, the greater the content to analyse using the tools in this book. An information-gathering style of questioning will help you to increase the content for indicators of deceptive language use. Asking the speaker to 'tell me what happened' is an effective approach to questioning.[57]

Keep your cards up your sleeve, bide your time, listen closely and stay alert.

## Overload a liar

It's not easy to lie. Liars have to work really hard when they do so: they need to come up with the lie, and then to monitor how it is landing. They need to anticipate the questions that may get asked. They need to remember everything they have said and who they have said it to. They need to get their demeanour right, appear honest and apply emotion if necessary. All the while, they need to keep monitoring the story and supplying instant clarifications that are coherent when questioned. And, while doing all this, they also need to suppress the truth.

It's quite a cognitive challenge! Making a liar's cognitive load even heavier can be used as an effective technique in lie detection.[58] There are various ways to do this in your role as the conversational partner.

THE LANGUAGE OF LIES

## 1. Ask unanticipated questions

Most of the time liars will have prepared answers to questions that they have anticipated. They will have thought through and memorised what they need to say in response to questions that they think someone may ask them. This means that liars are generally working from a scripted response. As we've explored, a scripted response runs chronologically and liars will try to keep to this ordering pattern. However, strategic questioning can cause a liar to slip up in their story. Asking unexpected questions, especially those to do with time or space, will greatly increase their cognitive load and might get them to make mistakes in their story.

Let's look at this high-stakes example from the murderer we discussed before. She is being interviewed by the police about her boyfriend's missing stepsister. She has already informed the police that she heard the victim leave the house, as she heard the front door slam while she was in the kitchen washing her hands. The detective then asks her the following unanticipated question:

**Police:** 'So how far away from the front door would you be?'

**Hoare:** 'Um [pause] but [pause] you've got the front door, living room then about halfway up the hallway [pause] is the kitchen so I would have been at the sink [pause] so [pause] don't know the distance, a reasonable amount [pause] I think.'[59]

She is unable to give a specific answer to this question. When we fabricate events, we generate them through the internal cognitive processes of reasoning and imagination. In other words, we are creating a simulation of an imagined experience. These simulations will lack specificity in temporal and spatial characteristics, unlike genuine memories which have much greater temporal and spatial detail.

In a criminal setting, like the one above, we can see how spatial questions can trip up liars, but what about in other situations? Spatial questions can take the form of asking how far away something or someone was; for example, how far away the hotel was from the train station, or how far the restaurant door was from the table.

Planned fabricated accounts are also less likely to use specific temporal words, such as 'days, weeks, years'.[60] Particularly when it comes to missing-person reports, this variation in language can be explained by the fact that genuine pleaders have a heightened awareness of how long the loved one has been missing, whereas fake pleaders might avoid using temporal details that are easily forgotten. Similarly, liars will avoid using numbers in their stories as remembering them requires a greater cognitive load.

Asking unexpected temporal questions will therefore put pressure on the liar. This is especially useful if you suspect the liar has prepared their story. For example, if you suspect that your partner was not, in fact, working late (but possibly having an affair), you might ask them questions such as: what time did you leave work, how many people were still there, what time train did you manage to catch, and so on. If your partner has a hard time answering these unexpected temporal questions, then you might want to investigate closer.

## 2. Ask the question again

Another effective questioning technique is repetition. Asking a question again a bit later will put the liar under cognitive strain and they might contradict themselves or display inconsistency. This is most effective if the liar has not had time to prepare their answer. The liar not only has to remember their prepared story, but also their earlier invented answer. A simple tip is when you repeat the question, try to ask it in a different way, so it does not immediately reveal that you are asking the same question.

Let's take the cheating partner scenario again. You've asked your partner what time they actually left work, and they were not prepared for this question and made something up. As this is a temporal question, it has already put them under cognitive strain. You then later ask them what train they managed to catch, or how long it took them to get home. If he or she is lying, they will need to remember what time they gave you earlier and then calculate what corresponding train they would have caught. Their answer becomes difficult to formulate and there will be a longer latency period.[61] Repeating your question can be an effective technique if you suspect you are being lied to.

## 3. Reverse the order

We can also increase a liar's cognitive load by asking questions that reverse the chronological ordering. Asking clarification questions that get the liar to start at the end of the story can be effective as it disrupts their invented sequential storytelling. Rather than asking: 'Then what happened?' ask: 'What happened before that?' This questioning technique disturbs the flow of events that the liar has invented, and they must work hard to reverse-recall their story, and will most likely slip up.

Like reverse-ordering questions, questions that disrupt the flow of the sequence will also lead to a higher cognitive load. For example, ask a question about something that happened in the middle of the tale, then ask about something at the start. Not following any chronological sequencing in your questioning will place the liar under cognitive strain and they are then likely to make mistakes.

## Fight fire with fire

Finally, I'm going to give you a piece of advice that might surprise you. With lies, sometimes there is no choice other than to fight fire with fire. When you are talking with skilled liars, amoral, manipulative and calculating individuals, then the most effective way to deal with their lies might be to lie in return. If they won't state the truth, then neither should you. Make things up. Confuse them. Tie them in knots. Invent things that *they* said, where *they* were, what *they* did, who *they* saw. Distort their story back to them. Make false claims. Deny, deflect and deceive. This tactic will cause a massive cognitive overload, as they will have to process how your lies conflict with the actual truth. Unsettle and unnerve them. Mirror their behaviour. Become a liar to catch a liar.

That cheating partner working late? Lie and say your friend saw them walking in the street with someone at the time they say they were at work. Your cheating partner now has to work very hard to remember where they were/were not walking and whether they were/were not with that person. Use an anonymous other. Someone told you, someone saw, someone heard. Similarly, if you have to prove your innocence because false claims are made about you, then throw some false claims back. Put your lying accuser into the same position they have put you in. Let them try to defend themselves against your false accusations.

A male colleague of one of my friends made false claims about her conduct and character to hide his own incompetence. She had to prove that she hadn't acted in that way and that she did not possess the characteristics she was being accused of. There were no witnesses. It was his lying words against her truthful ones. But rather than trying to prove her innocence and hope that it would be enough, she switched tactics, and she threw those same claims back at the accuser. *He* had acted like that, not her. She hadn't done what was alleged, *he* had done it. Now they were equal. If she had to defend herself against lies, then so should he. There was no other way to deal with such a lying and calculating individual but to join him. So she did, and she won. The claims against her were dropped. There was no way for the investigator to work out who was telling the truth, because neither of them was.

When we are faced with conflicting claims, it may be better to approach these claims from a position of trying to find out who is telling the lie rather than who is telling the truth. We usually search for the truth, but searching for lies in this situation may give us more of a critical perspective. We all need to take this critical perspective, particularly as it is down to us whether lies are believed or not. Not taking a critical perspective might have something to do with us being naturally lazy. We are more likely to believe false information as it takes less cognitive effort to believe a statement than to query the veracity of it.[62] This is because to query the veracity of something we have to work a bit harder by checking, critiquing, assessing and analysing the information. Alongside this the truth-bias is at work with our innate tendency to trust, rather than to distrust, what we are told. This causes us to accept any information as truthful in the first instance. How very vulnerable we all are!

But if we take a critical perspective to what others tell us, it will allow us to consider the goals and intentions behind what others say, which can in turn increase our lie detection ability: what hides behind their lies? What does the speaker achieve if they are lying? What do they want us to think about them, and why? What benefits do they get if we believe what they say? What is their personal investment if they are deceiving us?

Linguistic lie detection is not just knowing what types of language to watch out for; it is also being attentive to how you think and the things that you say in your interactions with others. With a suspected liar, learn to listen, be aware of the situational context, withhold judgements on emotional responses, accents and demeanour, pay close attention, don't be tricked by the truth, ask information-gathering questions and increase the cognitive load. These should all be added to your toolkit alongside what you now know to be the linguistic cues to lies and deception.

# Conclusion

At the beginning of this book, I told you about Caleb's girlfriend. I told you how the police initially followed her killer's lies about her murder being a suicide pact gone wrong. But perhaps if the police had had more understanding about how liars can reveal their lies in the language they use, they might not have trusted what they were told.

We may think (or hope) that people like the police are better at detecting lies than any of us, but they are not.[1] In fact, we are all equally vulnerable to being deceived. There is one group of people though who do appear to be better at detecting lies than most people and that's criminals.[2] Maybe by their nature they are familiar with the types of deceptive language used – they know what to be on the lookout for when a speaker says something. Or maybe it's because they are more wary of believing what they hear. Or it could be that they think most people are liars? Such might be their level of mistrust of others.

But I would urge you not to be so mistrusting. We are apt to jump to conclusions and to see what we want to see. Instead of being either trusting or untrusting, we should take a sober, balanced approach to what we hear. Before we point the finger at others, we need to critically assess, analyse and consider the many factors involved in linguistic lie detection. For instance, we should tread carefully as sometimes speakers who are vulnerable in some way (who have low IQ, high anxiety, memory or language deficits) may present with language which is more typical of liars, such as using more hesitations and longer response latency.

We should watch out also for individual linguistic differences amongst speakers who do not possess these vulnerabilities. There may be speakers who have a linguistic style that is lacking in sensory-perceptual words. It is difficult to adequately determine the likelihood that they are lying without considering what their normal linguistic style is. This is where having a good understanding of an individual's typical language use assists with lie detection. Being alert to where and when a speaker departs from their normal language use and style is vital.

You will also need to take into account whether the speaker has planned or prepared what they are going to say. This will help you to select the most appropriate linguistic cues to deceit that you should be watching out for, like pitch increases or lengthened lies. It could be that the speaker has not prepared their lies but is speaking spontaneously, and so you should focus on cues such as speech rate, repetition and filled pauses.

Think about what type of lying it could be. Is the

## CONCLUSION

speaker concealing information or their involvement in something? Or are they fabricating or inventing information? Lies of commission and omission can display different deceptive techniques in language. As we have seen, the length of a speaker's story can indicate fabricated parts, and pronoun use can help us spot invented identities like romance scammers. If a liar is omitting or hiding information or their culpability, then they may use distancing language. It's important to consider the type of lie you could be dealing with.

Keep in mind also that linguistic lie detection is easier when the speaker's motivation to lie is increased. When they have more to lose and the risks are high if their lies are not believed, these speakers' language can be littered with linguistic cues. As the stakes rise, so too does a liar's cognitive effort with the amount of remembering and constructing they must do, while also monitoring the listener or conversational partner's response and, when necessary, adapting what they are saying in real time. Their emotions such as guilt, fear, anxiety or excitement will also increase, and they have to keep these in check.

Being a liar is a complex cognitive task; they must do all this while also attempting to self-regulate their behaviour. There is no room for mistakes. But the mistakes will happen as language reflects our inner lives, thoughts and feelings;[3] hence linguistic cues to deceit will arise.

Your role as the listener or conversational partner in lie detection is easy in comparison with that of a speaker who is lying or concealing the truth. Follow the guidance you have been given throughout, don't forget to consider the situational context as you analyse the content of what a speaker says, and remember to increase the cognitive load when necessary.

Now that you understand the many ways that lies can be revealed through language, and the importance of your role, you are finally ready to detect a lie or two in your own life.

# Acknowledgements

I want to start by thanking my teacher in forensic linguistics – Dr John Olsson. I am enormously grateful to John for his training, his generosity in sharing his expertise and his critical encouragement of my own approach to the field. It is a deep sorrow to all who knew him and a huge loss to the field of forensic linguistics that John is no longer with us.

My great thanks to my wonderfully perceptive, wise and patient agent Michael Alcock for his constant encouragement and enthusiasm, and for his continued support and guidance. Special thanks to my dear friend Maxine Mei Fung Chung, whose advice and companionship throughout has been invaluable – thank you Max for always championing my work. My great appreciation is also for my gifted editor Anna Argenio, who crafted this book into superb shape. I am deeply indebted to Anna for her astute vision and incredible insight on initial drafts.

A huge thank you to Dr Karen Dwyer for our many years of talking all things linguistics, accompanying me to strange places on research trips, and for her expert advice on thought disorders and language. I am also very

## ACKNOWLEDGEMENTS

grateful to Nicholas Padfield KC for generously sharing his legal acuity with me at all hours and for his friendship, and to Mary Padfield for crafting Nicky's thoughts into copy. My thanks also to University College London who granted me the scholarship time in which to finish the book.

My sincere thanks to the team at Cornerstone, Penguin Random House, especially Kate Craigie for picking up the reins. And finally, I am deeply grateful to my family for all their support and for being my most patient audience – my mother Carol, my partner Jay and my dear daughter Lola.

# Notes

### INTRODUCTION

1. Forensic linguistics is not singularly focused on uncovering the deceptive use of language, but is a discipline that covers a wide range of areas such as authorship identification, plagiarism, language in evidence and the interpretation of meaning such as in legal terminology, and is an 'analysis of language that relates to the law, either as evidence or as legal discourse' (p. 1, Olsson, J., and Luchjenbroers, J. (2013) *Forensic Linguistics*. Bloomsbury, London and New York).
2. Pennebaker, J. W., and King, L. (1999) 'Linguistic styles: Language use as an individual difference'. *Journal of Personality and Social Psychology* 77(6), pp. 1296–1312.
3. Carey, A. L., Brucks, M. S., Küfner, A. C. P., Holtzman, N. S., Deters, F. G., Back, M. D., Donnellan, M. B., Pennebacker, J. W., and Mehl, M. R. (2015) 'Narcissism and the use of personal pronouns revisited'. *Journal of Personality and Social Psychology* 109(3), e1–e15.
4. Rude, S. S., Gortner, E. M., and Pennebaker, J. W. (2004) 'Language use of depressed and depressed-vulnerable college students'. *Cognition and Emotion* 18, pp. 1121–33.
5. Fineberg, S. K., Deutsch-Link, S., Ichinose, M., McGuinness, T., Bessette, A. J., Chung, C. K., and Corlett, P. R. (2015)

'Word use in first-person accounts of schizophrenia'. *British Journal of Psychiatry* 206(1), pp. 32–8.
6. Hartwig M., and Bond C. F. Jr. (2011) 'Why do lie-catchers fail? A lens model meta-analysis of human lie judgments'. *Psychological Bulletin* 137(4), pp. 643–59.
7. Bond, C. F. Jr., Omar, A., Mahmoud, A., and Bonser, R. N. (1990) 'Lie detection across cultures'. *Journal of Non-verbal Behavior* 14(3), pp. 189–204.
8. Mann, S., Vrij, A., and Bull, R. (2002) 'Suspects, lies, and videotape: An analysis of authentic high-stake liars'. *Law and Human Behavior* 26(3), pp. 365–76.
9. Wiseman, R., Watt, C., ten Brinke, L., Porter, S., Couper, S. L., and Rankin, C. (2012) 'The eyes don't have it: Lie detection and Neuro-Linguistic Programming'. *PLoS ONE* 7(7), e40259.
10. Tausczik, Y. R., and Pennebaker, J. W. (2010) 'The Psychological Meaning of Words: LIWC and Computerized Text Analysis Methods'. *Journal of Language and Social Psychology* 29, pp. 29, 24–54. http://dx.doi.org/10.1177/0261927X09351676
11. p. 111 of Coulthard, M. (1999) 'Forensic application of linguistic analysis', in Canter, D., and Alison, L. (eds.), *Interviewing and Deception*. Aldershot, England: Ashgate Publishing Ltd.
12. Dou, J., Liu, M., Muneer, H., and Schlussel, A. (n.d.) 'What words do we use to lie?: Word choice in deceptive messages'. Accessed at: https://arxiv.org/ftp/arxiv/papers/1710/1710.00273.pdf

# NOTES

## CHAPTER 1

1. https://www.thewrap.com/woody-allen-foolish-actors-boycott-persecuting-perfectly-innocent/
2. http://www.irishtimes.com/news/crime-and-law/jason-corbett-killing-recording-of-911-call-released-1.2489393
3. http://www.dailymail.co.uk/video/news/video-1077011/AUDIO-Moment-mother-LYING-MURDERER-son-calls-999.html
4. http://www.dailymail.co.uk/news/article-2854929/Mother-playboy-murdered-model-girlfriend-set-deported-Britain-covered-crime.html
5. http://www.journalnow.com/news/state_region/mother-says-she-was-asleep-when-child-disappeared/article_6589ad4f-16b9-5ff0-807f-17751632353b.html
6. https://www.youtube.com/watch?v=KXAzLfJX34A
7. http://www.news5cleveland.com/news/local-news/oh-lorain/lorain-missing-toddler-911-call-someone-grabbed-her-by-the-hand-and-ran-off-with-her
8. Hauch, V., Blandón-Gitlin, I., Masip, J., and Sporer, S. L. (2015) 'Are computers effective lie detectors? A meta-analysis of linguistic cues to deception'. *Personality and Social Psychology Review*, 19(4), pp. 307–42.
9. Johnson, M. K., Foley, M. A., Suengas, A. G., and Raye, C. L. (1988) 'Phenomenal characteristics of memories for perceived and imagined autobiographical events'. *Journal of Experimental Psychology: General* 117(4), pp. 371–6.

10. https://globalnews.ca/video/2757187/witness-inside-pulse-nightclub-describes-chaos-smell-of-ammunition
11. This scale is termed the Linguistic Category Model which is a model that identifies the nuances of how we use or choose certain language terms when we talk about social events or others. It gives information about how our verbal behaviour is driven by psychological processes and communication constraints. Semin, G. R., and Fiedler, K. (1988) 'The cognitive functions of linguistic categories in describing persons: Social cognition and language'. *Journal of Personality and Social Psychology* 54(4), pp. 558–68; Semin, G. R., and Fiedler, K. (1991) 'The linguistic category model, its bases, applications and range'. *European Review of Social Psychology* 2(1), pp. 1–30; Semin, G. R., and Fiedler, K. (1992) 'The inferential properties of interpersonal verbs', in Semin, G. R., and Fiedler, K. (eds.), *Language, Interaction and Social Cognition*. London: Sage Publications, pp. 58–78.
12. Semin, G. R. (1994) 'The linguistic category model and personality language', in Siegfried, J. (ed.), *The Status of Common Sense in Psychology*. Plenum Press, pp. 305–21.
13. Reitsma-van Rooijen, M., Semin, G. R., and van Leeuwen, E. (2007) 'The effect of linguistic abstraction on interpersonal distance'. *European Journal of Social Psychology* 37(5), pp. 817–23.
14. Schmid, J., Fiedler, K., Engich, B., Ehrenberger, T., and Semin, G. R. (1996) 'Taking sides with the defendant:

NOTES

Grammatical choice and the influence of implicit attributions in prosecution and defense speeches'. *International Journal of Psycholinguistics* 12(2), pp. 127–48.
15. Douglas, K., and Sutton, R. M. (2003) 'Effects of communication goals and expectancies on language abstraction'. *Journal of Personality and Social Psychology* 84(4), pp. 682–6.
16. *Junior Doctors* BBC Series 1, Episode 4, 'Your Life in their Hands': https://www.bbc.co.uk/programmes/b00zh82t#:~:text=Suzi's%20bedside%20manner%20is%20put,staff%20on%20the%20children's%20ward%3F
17. https://www.youtube.com/watch?v=QGTbx4PSfGE
18. https://www.youtube.com/watch?v=fiqTMcVL8Y0
19. Personal account taken from Huffington Post: https://www.huffingtonpost.co.uk/2014/12/16/boxing-day-tsunami-2004-thailand_n_6331872.html?guccounter=1&guce_referrer=aHR0cHM6Ly93d3cuZ29vZ2xlLmNvbS8&guce_referrer_sig=AQAAADKamCaaSrfAqu-ltSnoMLLuKr AHWiadUgzbNNtOFCqFc7WfS5iYJBePEwn59W-q06SWeMaTalaRUjWJ-20ahRkxSNVByoT8nmsj42y YZnHFJynsjotorYvBepd1569Xdz61qkNPMsDy6ul_teYQMyOU7-wPkBt9EKYEsOxR50YO
20. Taboo words in English usually refer to sex, sexual body parts and certain bodily functions and effluvia. Different languages have different categories of taboo words that may also consider as taboo those to do with diseases, death and killing, naming, addressing, touching and viewing persons and sacred beings, objects and places,

food gathering, preparation and consumption, and even in-laws! See Allan, K., and Burridge, K. (2007) *Forbidden Words: Taboo and the Censoring of Language.* Cambridge: Cambridge University Press.

21. It is well known that individuals are more likely to swear in response to feeling pain, and swearing has been confirmed as having a hypoalgesic effect – it can help to reduce the sensation of pain. See Stephens, R., Atkins, J., and Kingston, A. (2009) 'Swearing as a response to pain'. *NeuroReport* 20(12), pp. 1056–60.
22. Jay, T., and Janschewitz, K. (2008) 'The pragmatics of swearing'. *Journal of Politeness Research. Language, Behaviour, Culture* 4, pp. 267–88.
23. http://www.legislation.gov.uk/ukpga/1986/64
24. McEnery, T. (2004) *Swearing in English: Bad Language, Purity and Power from 1586 to the Present.* London: Routledge.
25. Jay, T. (1992) *Cursing in America: A psycholinguistic study of dirty language in the courts, in the movies, in the schoolyards and on the streets.* Amsterdam: John Benjamins.
26. Rassin, E., and Van Der Heijden, S. (2005) 'Appearing credible? Swearing helps!' *Psychology, Crime and Law* 11(2), pp. 177–82.
27. Feldman, G., Lian, H., Kosinski, M., and Stillwell, D. (2017) 'Frankly, we do give a damn: The relationship between profanity and honesty'. *Social Psychological and Personality Science.* First published date: 15 January 2017. DOI: 10.1177/1948550616681055.

28. Quotes taken from Egan, C. (2010) *Murderer No More: Andrew Mallard and the Epic Fight that Proved his Innocence*. Allen & Unwin Australia.
29. Truth-tellers were found to use more extreme swearing in their emergency calls, which was unexpected in the study by Burns, M. B., and Moffitt, K. C. (2014) 'Automated deception detection of 911 call transcripts'. *Security Informatics* 3(8), pp. 1–9.
30. Jay, T., and Janschewitz, K. (2008) 'The pragmatics of swearing'. *Journal of Politeness Research. Language, Behaviour, Culture* 4, pp. 267–88.
31. Inbau, F. E., Reid, J., Buckley, J., and Jayne, B. (2013) *Criminal interrogation and confessions* (5th edn). Burlington, MA: Jones & Bartlett.
32. Quote from Prendergast, Alan (1991) 'Wendy Bergen's Exclusive'. *American Journalism Review*. http://ajrarchive.org/article.asp?id=1504
33. Yates, P. M. (2009) 'Is sexual offender denial related to sex offence risk and recidivism? A review and treatment implications.' *Psychology, Crime and Law* 15(2–3), pp. 183–99.
34. https://torontosun.com/2016/05/27/the-gun-just-went-off-model-guilty-of-murdering-british-millionaire/wcm/16388958-cbb7-4cf7-93cb-1edc802ed38b
35. DePaulo, B. M., Lindsay, J. J., Malone, B. E., Muhlenbruck, L., Charlton, K., and Cooper, H. (2003) 'Cues to deception'. *Psychological Bulletin* 129(1), pp. 74–118.
36. http://www.dailymail.co.uk/video/news/video-1220730/Shauna-Hoare-gives-voluntary-witness-interview.html

37. Bolden, G. B. (2009) 'Beyond answering: Repeat-prefaced responses in conversation'. *Communication Monographs* 76(2), pp. 121–43.
38. https://www.youtube.com/watch?v=cmoO5UloOBI
39. Unkelbach, C. (2007) 'Reversing the truth effect: Learning the interpretation of processing fluency in judgments of truth'. *Journal of Experimental Psychology: Learning, Memory and Cognition* 33(1), pp. 219–30.
40. Unkelbach, C., Koch, A., Silva, R. R., and Garcia-Marques, T. (2019) 'Truth by Repetition: Explanations and Implications'. *Current Directions in Psychological Science* 28(3), pp. 247–53. https://doi.org/10.1177/0963721419827854
41. https://www.theguardian.com/sport/2013/jan/18/lance-armstrong-doping-denials-quotes
42. https://www.theguardian.com/uk-news/2018/sep/13/russian-television-channel-rt-says-it-is-to-air-interview-with-skripal-salisbury-attack-suspects
43. Van Swol, L. M., Braun, M. T., and Malhotra, D. (2012) 'Evidence for the Pinocchio effect: Linguistic differences between lies, deception by omissions, and truths'. *Discourse Processes* 49, pp. 79–106.
44. Hancock, J. T., Curry, L. E., Goorha, S., and Woodworth, M. (2008) 'On lying and being lied to: A linguistic analysis of deception in computer-mediated communication'. *Discourse Processes* 45(1), pp. 1–23.
45. http://nationalreport.net/15-year-old-swatted-domestic-terrorism/

NOTES

46. http://www.kptv.com/story/28287845/police-release-disturbing-911-swatting-calls
47. https://www.youtube.com/watch?v=yzRkco6TNi8
48. http://www.orlandosentinel.com/news/breaking-news/orlnews-911-audio-swatting-hoax-a-20140812-embeddedvideo.html
49. Nes, A. (2016) 'Assertion, belief, and "I believe" guarded affirmation'. *Linguistics and Philosophy* 39(1), pp. 57–86.
50. http://www.nytimes.com/1994/04/15/us/tobacco-chiefs-say-cigarettes-aren-t-addictive.html?pagewanted=all&src=pm
51. Henningfield, J. E., Rose, C. A., and Zeller, M. (2006) 'Tobacco industry litigation position on addiction: Continued dependence on past views'. *Tobacco Control* 15 (Suppl 4), pp. iv27–iv36.
52. https://www.latimes.com/la-me-ln-san-diego-ph-miracle-lawsuit-20181102-story.html
53. Helgason, B. A., and Effron, D. A. (2022) 'It might become true: How prefactual thinking licenses dishonesty'. *Journal of Personality and Social Psychology* 123(5), pp. 909–40. https://doi.org/10.1037/pspa0000308
54. Clifford, W. K. (1877) [1999], 'The Ethics of Belief', in Madigan, T. (ed.), *The Ethics of Belief and Other Essays*, Amherst, MA: Prometheus, pp. 70–96.

CHAPTER 2

1. Leslie, A. M. (1982) 'The perception of causality in infants'. *Perception* 11(2), pp. 173–86; Mandler, J. M. (1992) 'How

to build a baby II: Conceptual primitives'. *Psychological Review* 99(4), pp. 587–604.
2. Williams, L. E., and Bargh, J. A. (2008) 'Keeping one's distance: The influence of spatial distance cues on affect and evaluation'. *Psychological Science* 19(3), pp. 302–8.
3. Baltatescu, S. (2014) 'Psychological distance', in Michalos, A. C. (ed.), *Encyclopedia of Quality of Life and Well-Being Research*. Springer, Dordrecht, pp. 5145–6.
4. Van Boven, L., and Caruso, E. M. (2015) 'The tripartite foundations of temporal psychological distance: Metaphors, ecology and teleology'. *Social and Personality Psychology Compass* 9(11), pp. 593–605.
5. Williams, L. E., and Bargh, J. A. (2008) 'Keeping one's distance: The influence of spatial distance cues on affect and evaluation'. *Psychological Science* 19(3), pp. 302–8.
6. Kross, E., Ayduk, O., and Mischel, W. (2005) 'When asking "why" does not hurt. Distinguishing rumination from reflective processing of negative emotion'. *Psychological Science* 16(9), pp. 709–15.
7. Eibach, R. P., Libby, L. K., and Gilovich, T. (2003) 'When change in the self is mistaken for change in the world'. *Journal of Personality and Social Psychology* 84(5), pp. 917–31.
8. Pronin, E., and Ross, L. (2006) 'Temporal differences in trait self-ascription: When the self is seen as an other'. *Journal of Personality and Social Psychology* 90(2), pp. 197–209.
9. Wiener, M., and Mehrabian, A. (1968) *Language within language: Immediacy, a channel in verbal communication*. New York: Appleton-Century-Crofts.

10. p. 33 of Wiener, M., and Mehrabian, A. (1968) *Language within language: Immediacy, a channel in verbal communication*. New York: Appleton-Century-Crofts. Carrera, P., Muñoz, D., Caballero, A., Fernández, I., Aguilar, P., and Albarracín, D. (2014) 'How verb tense affects the construal of action: The simple past tense leads people into an abstract mindset'. *Psicológica* 35(2), pp. 209–23.
11. Brysbaert, M., Stevens, M., Mandera, P., and Keuleers, E. (2016) 'How many words do we know? Practical estimates of vocabulary size dependent on word definition, the degree of language input and the participant's age'. *Frontiers in Psychology*, 29 July 2016;7:1116. doi: 10.3389/fpsyg.2016.01116.
12. Rochon, E., Saffran, E. M., Berndt, R. S., and Schwartz, M. F. (2000) 'Quantitative analysis of aphasic sentence production: Further development and new data'. *Brain and Language* 72(3), pp. 193–218.
13. Newman, M. L., Pennebaker, J. W., Berry, D. S., and Richards, J. M. (2003) 'Lying words: Predicting deception from linguistic style'. *Personality and Social Psychology Bulletin* 29(5), pp. 665–75.
14. Lee, C., Welker, R. B., and Odom, M. B. (2009) 'Features of computer-mediated text-based messages that support automatable, linguistics-based indicators for deception detection'. *Journal of Information Systems* 23, pp. 5–24.
15. Newman, M. L., Pennebaker, J. W., Berry, D. S., and Richards, J. M. (2003) 'Lying words: Predicting deception

from linguistic styles'. *Personality and Social Psychology Bulletin* 29(5), pp. 665–75.
16. https://www.theguardian.com/uk-news/video/2017/feb/22/ian-stewart-999-call-helen-bailey-murder-missing-audio
17. Anthony Weiner interview with Wolf Blitzer, 1 June 2011, https://www.youtube.com/watch?v=xeiIOzFPsqg
18. While the data from these studies comes from written communications, we should expect to see the same differences in pronominal usage in verbal communication as the intent of deceptive relationship building would be the same. Lee, K.-F., Chan, M. Y., and Mohamad Ali, A. (2023) 'Self and desired partner descriptions in the online romance scam: A linguistic analysis of scammer and general user profiles on online dating portals'. *Crime Prevention and Community Safety* 25(1), pp. 20–46.
19. Baryshevtsev, M., and McGlone, M. S. (2018) 'Pronoun usage in online sexual predation'. *Cyberpsychology, Behavior, and Social Networking* 21(2), pp. 117–22.
20. Federal Trade Commission (2022) 'Reports of romance scams hit record highs in 2021'. Consumer Protection Data Spotlight. Available at: https://www.ftc.gov/system/files/ftc_gov/pdf/romance_spotlight_final_february_2022.pdf
21. This real data is taken from Beek, J. (2018) 'How not to fall in love: Mistrust in online romance scams', in Mühlfried, F. (ed.), *Mistrust: Ethnographic Approximations*. De Gruyter, pp. 49–70. It is from a textual account rather than spoken and has been edited for readability, e.g. 'you' instead of 'u'.

22. Ickes, W., Reidhead, S., and Patterson, M. (1986) 'Machiavellianism and self-monitoring: As different as "me" and "you"'. *Social Cognition* 4(1), pp. 58–74.
23. Ickes, W. (2010) 'Self-Monitoring', *Strangers in a Strange Lab: How Personality Shapes Our Initial Encounters with Others* (New York, 2009; online edn, Oxford Academic, 1 April 2010), https://doi.org/10.1093/acprof:oso/9780195372953.003.0010
24. Ickes, W., Reidhead, S., and Patterson, M. (1986) 'Machiavellianism and self-monitoring: As different as "me" and "you"'. *Social Cognition* 4(1), pp. 58–74.
25. Henley, N. M., Miller, M., and Beazley, J. A. (1995) 'Syntax, semantics, and sexual violence: Agency and the passive voice'. *Journal of Language and Social Psychology* 14(1/2), pp. 60–84.
26. Coates, L., and Wade, A. (2004) 'Telling it like it isn't: Obscuring perpetrator responsibility for violent crime'. *Discourse & Society* 15(5), pp. 499–526.
27. Ehrlich, S. (2001) *Representing Rape: Language and Sexual Consent*. London: Routledge.
28. https://www.standard.co.uk/news/london/dogs-shot-man-tasered-metropolitan-police-limehouse-canal-london-crime-b1079532.html
29. Chan, E. Y., and Maglio, S. J. (2020) 'The voice of cognition: Active and passive voice influence distance and construal'. *Personality and Social Psychology Bulletin* 46(4), pp. 547–58.

30. Sato, S. (2008) 'Use of "please" in American and New Zealand English'. *Journal of Pragmatics* 40(7), pp. 1249–78.
31. Wichmann, A. (2004) 'The intonation of please-requests: A corpus-based study'. *Journal of Pragmatics* 36(9), pp. 1521–49.
32. Woods, R. (2015) 'Modelling the syntax-discourse interface: A syntactic analysis of *please*', paper presented at ConSOLE XXIII, Université Paris Diderot-Paris VII, 8 January 2015.
33. http://www.orlandosentinel.com/news/breaking-news/os-pit-bull-attack-sanford-audio-20160121-story.html
34. https://www.thestar.com/news/2014/04/24/jennifer_pan_911_call.html
35. Stephan, E., Liberman, N., and Trope, Y. (2010) 'Politeness and psychological distance: A construal level perspective'. *Journal of Personality and Social Psychology* 98(2), pp. 268–80.
36. https://www.nytimes.com/2018/09/17/obituaries/alan-abel-dies.html
37. Carrera, P., Munoz, D., Caballero, A., Fernández, I, Aguilar, P., and Albarracín, D. (2014) 'How verb tense affects the construal of action: The simple past tense leads people into an abstract mindset'. *Psicológica* 35(2), pp. 209–23.
38. https://www.youtube.com/watch?v=WiNMbCvc5Sk
39. https://www.youtube.com/watch?v=xioriPZaOAA
40. Hart, W., and Albarracín, D. (2011) 'Learning about what others were doing: Verb aspect and attributions of mundane and criminal intent for past actions'. *Psychological Science* 22(2), pp. 261–6.
41. Sherrill, A. M., Eerland, A., Zwaan, R. A., and Magliano, J. P. (2015) 'Understanding how grammatical aspect

influences legal judgment'. *PLoS ONE*: https://doi.org/10.1371/journal.pone.0141181

42. Gandolfi, G., Pickering, M. J., and Garrod, S. (2023) 'Mechanisms of alignment: Shared control, social cognition and metacognition'. *Philosophical Transactions of the Royal Society* B 378 (1870).
43. http://www.mirror.co.uk/news/uk-news/i-did-not-murder-falconio-567159
44. https://www.thesun.co.uk/video/news/police-release-interview-footage-of-paul-hemming-before-murder-sentence/
45. Bernieri, F. J. (1988) 'Coordinated movement and rapport in teacher-student interactions'. *Journal of Nonverbal Behavior* 12(2), pp. 120–38.
46. Levelt, W. J., and Kelter, S. (1982) 'Surface form and memory in question answering'. *Cognitive Psychology* 14(1), pp. 78–106.
47. Garrod, S., and Anderson, A. (1987) 'Saying what you mean in dialogue: A study in conceptual and semantic co-ordination'. *Cognition* 27(2), pp. 181–218; Pickering, M. J., and Garrod, S. (2004) 'Toward a mechanistic psychology of dialogue'. *Behavioral and Brain Sciences* 27(2), pp. 169–226.
48. Taylor, P. J., Dando, C. J., Ormerod, T. C, Ball, L. J., Jenkins, M. C., Sandham, A., and Menacere, T. (2013) 'Detecting insider threats through language change'. *Law and Human Behaviour* 37(4), pp. 267–75.
49. https://www.youtube.com/watch?v=L6-kxlrwuc8

50. Repke, M. A., Conway, L. G., and Houck, S. C. (2018) 'The strategic manipulation of linguistic complexity: A test of two models of lying'. *Journal of Language and Social Psychology* 37(1), pp. 74–92. https://doi.org/10.1177/0261927X17706943. This study investigates decreases and increases in complexity and finds that both appear but that the speaker's goal is important in the difference, such that strategic goals will give rise to increases in complexity, but stress and the social context cause decreases. See also Duran, N. D., Hall, C., McCarthy, P. M., and McNamara, D. S. (2010) 'The Linguistic correlates of conversational deception: Comparing natural language processing technologies'. *Applied Psycholinguistics* 31, pp. 439–62. DePaulo, B. M., Lindsay, J. J., Malone, B. E., Muhlenbruck, L., Charlton, K., and Cooper, H. (2003) 'Cues to deception'. *Psychological Bulletin* 129(1), pp. 74–118.
51. Zhou, L., Burgoon, J. K., Nunamaker, J. F., and Twitchell, D. P. (2004) 'Automating linguistic-based cues for detecting deception in text-based asynchronous computer-mediated communication'. *Group Decision and Negotiation* 13(1), pp. 81–106.
52. Newman, M. L., Pennebaker, J. W., Berry, D. S., and Richards, J. M. (2003) 'Lying words: Predicting deception from linguistic styles'. *Personality and Social Psychology Bulletin* 29, pp. 665–75.
53. Zhou, L., Burgoon, J. K., Nunamaker, J. F., and Twitchell, D. P. (2004) 'Automating linguistic-based cues for detecting

deception in text-based asynchronous computer-mediated communication'. *Group Decision and Negotiation* 13(1), pp. 81–106.

54. This study finds that liars used fewer words – ten Brinke, L., and Porter, S. (2012) 'Cry me a river: Identifying the behavioral consequences of extremely high-stakes interpersonal deception'. *Law and Human Behavior* 36(6), pp. 469–77.

55. Vrij, A., Mann, S. A., Fisher, R. P., Leal, S., Milne, R., and Bull, R. (2008) 'Increasing cognitive load to facilitate lie detection: The benefit of recalling an event in reverse order'. *Law and Human Behavior* 32(3), 253–265. doi:10.1007/s10979-007-9103-y

56. Labov, W. (1997) 'Some further steps in narrative analysis'. *Journal of Narrative and Life History* 7(1–4), pp. 395–415.

57. Labov, W., and Waletsky, J. (1967) 'Narrative analysis: Oral versions of personal experience', in Helm, J. (ed.), *Essays on the Verbal and Visual Arts: Proceedings of the 1966 Annual Spring Meeting of the American Ethnological Society*. Seattle: University of Washington Press, pp. 12–44.

58. Thorndyke, P. W. (1977) 'Cognitive structures in comprehension and memory of narrative discourse'. *Cognitive Psychology* 9(1), pp. 77–110.

59. https://www.youtube.com/watch?v=Mz5aL8JDzDg

60. Pennington, N., and Hastie, R. (1986) 'Evidence evaluation in complex decision making'. *Journal of Personality and Social Psychology* 51(2), pp. 242–58; Canter, D. V., Grieve,

N., Nicol, C., and Benneworth, K. (2003) 'Narrative plausibility: The impact of sequence and anchoring'. *Behavioral Sciences & the Law* 21(2), pp. 251–67.

61. Vrij, A., Mann, S. A., Fisher, R. P., Leal, S., Milne, R., and Bull, R. (2008) 'Increasing cognitive load to facilitate lie detection: The benefit of recalling an event in reverse order'. *Law and Human Behavior* 32(3), pp. 253–65.

62. DePaulo, B. M., Lindsay, J. J., Malone, B. E., Muhlenbruck, L., Charlton, K., and Cooper, H. (2003) 'Cues to deception'. *Psychological Bulletin* 129(1), pp. 74–118.

63. DePaulo, B. M., Rosenthal, R., Rosenkrantz, J., and Green, C. R. (1982) 'Actual and perceived cues to deception: A closer look at speech'. *Basic and Applied Social Psychology* 3(4), pp. 291–312; Akehurst, L., Köhnken, G., Vrij, A., and Bull, R. (1996) 'Lay persons' and police officers' beliefs regarding deceptive behaviour'. *Applied Cognitive Psychology* 10(6), pp. 461–71; Vrij, A., Evans, H., Akehurst, L., and Mann, S. (2004) 'Rapid judgements in assessing verbal and nonverbal cues: Their potential for deception researchers and lie detection'. *Applied Cognitive Psychology* 18(3), pp. 283–96; Vrij, A. (2008) 'Nonverbal dominance versus verbal accuracy in lie detection: A plea to change police practice'. *Criminal Justice and Behavior* 35(10), pp. 1323–36.

64. Van Swol, L. M., Braun, M. T., and Malhotra, D. (2012) 'Evidence for the Pinocchio effect: Linguistic differences between lies, deception by omissions, and truths'. *Discourse Processes* 49(2), pp. 79–106.

NOTES

65. Burgoon, J. K., and Qin, T. (2006) 'The dynamic nature of deceptive verbal communication'. *Journal of Language and Social Psychology* 25(1), pp. 76–96.
66. Johnson, M. K., Foley, M. A., Suengas, A. G., and Raye, C. L. (1988) 'Phenomenal characteristics of memories for perceived and imagined autobiographical events'. *Journal of Experimental Psychology* 117(4), pp. 371–76.
67. https://www.youtube.com/watch?v=pXLx5OY21Bk
68. https://www.youtube.com/watch?v=SLWSI8-rkIs
69. Van Swol, L. M., Braun, M. T., and Malhotra, D. (2012) 'Evidence for the Pinocchio effect: Linguistic differences between lies, deception by omissions, and truths'. *Discourse Processes* 49(2), pp. 79–106.

CHAPTER 3

1. Some research proposes that using all available communication channels, verbal and paraverbal together, improves deception detection. Archer, D., and Lansley, C. (2015) 'Public appeals, news interviews and crocodile tears: An argument for multi-channel analysis'. *Corpora* 10(2), pp. 231–58. DOI: http://dx.doi.org/10.3366/cor.2015.0075
2. For a brief review of how this stands in law, see Miller, G. (2024) 'The devil made me do it: The viability of demonic possession as a murder defense'. *Vermont Law Review* (online): https://lawreview.vermontlaw.edu/the-devil-made-me-do-it-the-viability-of-demonic-possession-as-a-murder-defense/#_ftn13

3. Biemiller, A., and Slonim, N. (2001) 'Estimating root word vocabulary growth in normative and advantaged populations: Evidence for a common sequence of vocabulary acquisition'. *Journal of Educational Psychology* 93(3), pp. 498–520.
4. Lust, B. (2006) *Child Language: Acquisition and Growth*. Cambridge: Cambridge University Press.
5. Hughes, S. M., and Rhodes, B. C. (2010) 'Making age assessments based on voice: The impact of the reproductive viability of the speaker'. *Journal of Social, Evolutionary and Cultural Psychology* 4(4), pp. 290–304.
6. Bezooijen, R. V. (1984) *The Characteristics and Recognizability of Vocal Expressions of Emotions*. Berlin, Boston: De Gruyter Mouton.
7. Pell, M. D., Monetta, L., Paulmann, S., and Kotz, S. A. (2009) 'Recognizing emotions in a foreign language'. *Journal of Nonverbal Behavior* 33(2), pp. 107–20. doi: 10.1007/s10919-008-0065-7.
8. Asghari, S. Z., Farashi, S., Bashirian, S., et al. (2021) 'Distinctive prosodic features of people with autism spectrum disorder: A systematic review and meta-analysis study'. *Science Report* 11(1). https://doi.org/10.1038/s41598-021-02487-6
9. Leff, J., and Abberton, E. (1981) 'Voice pitch measurements in schizophrenia and depression'. *Psychological Medicine* 11(4), pp. 849–52.
10. Compton, M. T., Lunden, A., Cleary, S. D., Pauselli, L., Alolayan, Y., Halpern, B., et al. (2018) 'The aprosody of

schizophrenia: Computationally derived acoustic phonetic underpinnings of monotone speech'. *Schizophrenia Research* 197, pp. 392–9. https://doi.org/10.1016/j.schres.2018.01.007 Cummins, N., Sethu, V., Epps, J., Schnieder, S., and Krajewski, J. (2015) 'Analysis of acoustic space variability in speech affected by depression'. *Speech Communication* 75, pp. 27–49. https://doi.org/10.1016/j.specom.2015.09.003.

11. McCutcheon, R. A., Keefe, R. S. E., and McGuire, P. K. (2023) 'Cognitive impairment in schizophrenia: Aetiology, pathophysiology, and treatment'. *Molecular Psychiatry* 28(5), pp. 1902–18. https://doi.org/10.1038/s41380-023-01949-9. McIntyre, R. S., Cha, D. S., Soczynska, J. K., et al. (2013) 'Cognitive deficits and functional outcomes in major depressive disorder: Determinants, substrates, and treatment interventions'. *Depression and Anxiety* 30(6), pp. 515–27.

12. Berardi, M., Brosch, K., Pfarr, J. K., et al. (2023) 'Relative importance of speech and voice features in the classification of schizophrenia and depression'. *Translational Psychiatry* 13(1), article 298, https://doi.org/10.1038/s41398-023-02594-0

13. Bagley, A. D., Abramowitz, C. S., and Kosson, D. S. (2009) 'Vocal affect recognition and psychopathy: Converging findings across traditional and cluster analytic approaches to assessing the construct'. *Journal of Abnormal Psychology* 118(2), pp. 388–98.

14. Sell, A., Bryant, G. A., Cosmides, L., Tooby, J., Sznycer, D., et al. (2010) 'Adaptations in humans for assessing physical

strength from the voice'. *Proceedings of the Royal Society B: Biological Sciences* 277(1699), pp. 3509–18.

15. Feinberg, D. R., Jones, B. C., Little, A. C., Burt, D. M., and Perrett, D. I. (2005) 'Manipulations of fundamental and formant frequencies influence the attractiveness of human male voices'. *Animal Behaviour* 69(3), pp. 561–8.
16. Wolff, S. E., and Puts, D. A. (2010) 'Vocal masculinity is a robust dominance signal in men'. *Behavioral Ecology and Sociobiology* 64(10), pp. 1673–83.
17. Feinberg, D. R., DeBruine, L. M., Jones, B. C., and Perrett, D. I. (2008) 'The role of femininity and averageness of voice pitch in aesthetic judgments of women's voices'. *Perception* 37(4), pp. 615–23. doi: 10.1068/p5514. PMID: 18546667.
18. Imhof, M. (2010) 'Listening to voices and judging people'. *International Journal of Listening* 24(1), pp. 19–33.
19. Klofstad, C. A., Anderson R. C., and Nowicki S. (2015) 'Perceptions of competence, strength, and age influence voters to select leaders with lower-pitched voices'. *PLoS ONE* 10(8), e0133779. doi:10.1371/journal.pone.0133779).
20. Anolli, L., and Ciceri, R. (1997) 'The voice of deception: Vocal strategies of naïve and able liars'. *Journal of Nonverbal Behaviour* 21(4), pp. 259–84. Sporer, S. L., and Schwandt, B. (2006) 'Paraverbal indicators of deception: A meta-analytic synthesis'. *Applied Cognitive Psychology* 20(4), pp. 421–46.
21. Cardoso, R., Lumini-Oliveira, J., and Meneses, R. F. (2021) 'Associations between autonomic nervous system function, voice, and dysphonia: A systematic review'.

*Journal of Voice* 35(1), pp. 104–12, https://doi.org/10.1016/j.jvoice.2019.07.022
22. Jiang, X., and Pell, M. D. (2017) 'The sound of confidence and doubt'. *Speech Communication* 88, pp. 106–26.
23. Krishnamurthy, R., and Ramani, S. A. (2020) 'Aerodynamic and acoustic characteristics of voice in children with down syndrome: A systematic review'. *International Journal of Pediatric Otorhinolaryngology* 133, article 109946, https://doi.org/10.1016/j.ijporl.2020.109946
24. Scherer, K. R. (1985) 'Methods of research on vocal communication: Paradigms and parameters', in Scherer, K. R., and Ekman P. (eds.), *Handbook of Methods in Nonverbal Behavior Research*. Cambridge: CUP, pp. 136–98; Rockwell, P., Buller, D. B., and Burgoon, J. K. (1997) 'The voice of deceit: Refining and expanding vocal cues to deception'. *Communication Research Reports* 14(4), pp. 451–59.
25. https://www.youtube.com/watch?v=bbSaFP_oNEc
26. http://www.mirror.co.uk/news/uk-news/pc-made-hoax-call-force-7701663
27. Vrij, A., Edward, K., and Bull, R. (2001) 'Stereotypical verbal and nonverbal responses while deceiving others'. *Personality and Social Psychology Bulletin* 27(7), pp. 899–909.
28. Fiedler, K., and Walka, I. (1993) 'Training lie detectors to use nonverbal cues instead of global heuristics'. *Human Communication Research* 20(2), pp. 199–223; Rockwell, P., Buller, D. B., and Burgoon, J. K. (1997) 'The voice

of deceit: Refining and expanding vocal cues to deception'. *Communication Research Reports* 14(4), pp. 451–59.
29. Speech rate can be a very difficult indicator as it is very difficult to quantify. Most studies which look at speech rate and deception analyse English, although other languages are not structured in the same way. Therefore, other languages may have shorter words which increases the rate of speech, or they may have longer words and the rate decreases.
30. Mehrabian, A. (1971) 'Nonverbal betrayal of feeling'. *Journal of Experimental Research in Personality* 5(1), pp. 64–73. Buller, D. B., and Aune, R. K. (1987) 'Nonverbal cues to deception among intimates, friends and strangers'. *Journal of Nonverbal Behavior* 11(4), pp. 269–90.
31. Loveday, L. (1981) 'Pitch, politeness and sexual role: An exploratory investigation into the pitch correlates of English and Japanese politeness formulae'. *Language and Speech* 24(1), pp. 71–89.
32. Schlenker, B. R. (1980) *Impression Management: The self-concept, social identity, and interpersonal relations*. Monterey, CA: Brooks / Cole.
33. Barr, D. J. (2003) 'Paralinguistic correlates of conceptual structure'. *Psychonomic Bulletin & Review* 10(2), pp. 462–7; Jiang, X., and Pell, M. D. (2015) 'On how the brain decodes vocal cues about speaker confidence'. *Cortex* 66, pp. 9–34.

34. http://www.dailymotion.com/video/xc8x6d_911-audio-mi-woman-calls-911-report_news
35. Lickley, R. (1995) 'Missing disfluencies'. *Proceedings, International Congress of Phonetic Sciences* 4, pp. 192–5. Stockholm.
36. Merlo, S., and Mansur, L. L. (2004) 'Descriptive discourse: Topic familiarity and disfluencies'. *Journal of Communication Disorders* 37(6), pp. 489–503.
37. Swerts, M., and Krahmer, E. (2005) 'Audiovisual prosody and feeling of knowing'. *Journal of Memory and Language* 53(1), pp. 81–94. Christenfeld, N., and Creager, B. (1996) 'Anxiety, alcohol, aphasia, and ums'. *Journal of Personality and Social Psychology* 70(3), pp. 451–60.
38. Clark, H. H., and Fox Tree, J. E. (2002) 'Using uh and um in spontaneous speaking'. *Cognition* 84(1), pp. 73–111.
39. Arciuli, J., Mallard, D., and Villar, G. (2010) ' "Um, I can tell you're lying": Linguistic markers of deception versus truth-telling in speech'. *Applied Psycholinguistics* 31(3), pp. 397–411. doi: 10.1017/S0142716410000044.
40. Wieling, M., Grieve, J., Bouma, G., Fruehwald, J., Coleman, J., and Liberman, M. (2016) 'Variation and change in the use of hesitation markers in Germanic languages'. *Language Dynamics and Change* 6(2), pp. 199–234. https://doi.org/10.1163/22105832-00602001
41. Villar, G., Arciuli, J., and Mallard, D. (2012) 'Use of "um" in the deceptive speech of a convicted murderer'. *Applied Psycholinguistics* 33(1), pp. 83–95.

NOTES

42. Loy, J. E., Rohde, H., and Corley, M. (2018) 'Cues to lying may be deceptive: Speaker and listener behaviour in an interactive game of deception'. *Journal of Cognition* 1(1):42. doi: 10.5334/joc.46.
43. Vrij, A., and Heaven, S. (1999) 'Vocal and verbal indicators of deception as a function of lie complexity'. *Psychology, Crime & Law* 5(3), pp. 203–15.
44. Christenfeld, N., and Creager, B. (1996) 'Anxiety, alcohol, aphasia, and ums'. *Journal of Personality and Social Psychology* 70(3), pp. 451–60. doi: 10.1037//0022-3514.70.3.451.
45. Vrij, A., Edward, K., and Bull, R. (2001) 'Stereotypical verbal and nonverbal responses while deceiving others'. *Personality and Social Psychology Bulletin* 27(7), pp. 899–909. DOI: 10.1177/0146167201277012.
46. https://www.youtube.com/watch?v=3I19Zk9htSc
47. Rochester, S. R. (1973) 'The significance of pauses in spontaneous speech'. *Journal of Psycholinguistic Research* 2(1), pp. 51–81.
48. Kasl, S., and Mahl, G. (1965) 'The relationship of disturbances and hesitations in spontaneous speech to anxiety'. *Journal of Personality and Social Psychology* 1(5), pp. 425–33; Ragsdale, J. D. (1976) 'Relationship between hesitation phenomena, anxiety and self-control in a normal communication situation'. *Language and Speech* 19(3), pp. 257–65.
49. p. 85 of Feldstein, S., Alberti, L., and BenDebba, M. (1979) 'Self-attributed personality characteristics and the pacing of conversational interaction', in Siegman, Aron W., and

Feldstein, Stanley (eds.), *Of Speech and Time: Temporal Speech Patterns in Interpersonal Contexts*. Hillsdale, New Jersey: Lawrence Erlbaum Associates, pp. 73–88.
50. Mann, S., Vrij, A., and Bull, R. (2002) 'Suspects, lies, and videotape: An analysis of authentic high-stake liars'. *Law and Human Behavior* 26(3), pp. 365–76.
51. Cappella, J. (1985) 'Controlling the floor in conversation', in Siegman, Aron W., and Feldstein, Stanley (eds.), *Multichannel Integrations of Nonverbal Behavior*. New York and London: Psychology Press, pp. 69–104.
52. https://www.youtube.com/watch?v=2a5A7scBx4k
53. Maclay, H., and Osgood, C. E. (1959) 'Hesitation phenomena in spontaneous English speech'. *Word* 15(1), pp. 19–44.
54. Research has also proposed that response latency is related to upcoming 'trouble', and the context in which response latency arises is important, see Reynolds, E., and Rendle-Short, J. (2011) 'Cues to deception in context: Response latency/gaps in denials and blame shifting'. *British Journal of Social Psychology* 50(3), pp. 431–49.
55. Stivers, T., Enfield, N. J., Brown, P., Englert, C., Hayashi, M., Heinemann, T., et al. (2009) 'Universals and cultural variation in turn-taking in conversation'. *Proceedings of the National Academy of Sciences, USA* 106(26), pp. 10587–92. doi: 10.1073/pnas.0903616106.
56. Sacks, H., Schegloff, E. A., and Jefferson, G. (1974) 'A simplest systematics for the organization of turn-taking for conversation'. *Language* 50(4), pp. 696–735. doi: 10.2307/412243.

57. Sporer, S. L., and Schwandt, B. (2006) 'Paraverbal indicators of deception: A meta analytic synthesis'. *Applied Cognitive Psychology* 20(4), pp. 421–46. Vrij, A. (2008) 'Statement validity assessment', in *Detecting Lies and Deceit: Pitfalls and Opportunities* (2nd edn, pp. 201–61). Chichester: Wiley.
58. Walczyk, J. J., Roper, K. S., Seemann, E., and Humphrey A. M. (2003) 'Cognitive mechanisms underlying lying to questions: Response time as a cue to deception'. *Applied Cognitive Psychology* 17(7), pp. 755–74.
59. Williams, E. J., Bott, L. A., Patrick, J., and Lewis, M. B. (2013) 'Telling lies: The irrepressible truth?' *PLoS ONE* 8(4). e60713.
60. Zuckerman, M., DePaulo, B. M., and Rosenthal, R. (1981) 'Verbal and nonverbal communication of deception', in Berkowitz, L. (ed.), *Advances in Experimental Social Psychology*, vol. 14. New York: Academic Press, pp. 1–59.
61. https://www.youtube.com/watch?v=3I19Zk9htSc
62. Responses to polar questions (yes/no questions) are generally faster than responses to content questions in non-lying responses as well. Strömbergsson, S., Hjalmarsson, A., Edlund, J., and House, D. (2013) 'Timing responses to questions in dialogue', in *Proceedings of Interspeech* 2013, (Lyon: International Speech Communication Association), pp. 2584–8.
63. Walczyk, J. J., Schwartz, J. P., Clifton, R., Adams, B., Wei, M., et al. (2005) 'Lying person-to-person about life

events: A cognitive framework for lie detection'. *Personnel Psychology* 58(1), pp. 141–70.
64. https://www.youtube.com/watch?v=xcRIS_zIklo
65. See Vrij, A. (2008) *Detecting Lies and Deceit: Pitfalls and Opportunities* (2nd edn). New York: Wiley, who reviews the studies that conclude more speech errors are found in liars' speech.
66. Kasl, S. V., and Mahl, G. F. (1965) 'The relationship of disturbances and hesitations in spontaneous speech to anxiety'. *Journal of Personality and Social Psychology* 1(5), pp. 425–33.
67. https://www.youtube.com/watch?v=W-l2f7TWZjs

CHAPTER 4

1. Vrij, A., Granhag, P. A., and Porter, S. (2010) 'Pitfalls and opportunities in nonverbal and verbal lie detection'. *Psychological Science in the Public Interest* 11(3), pp. 89–121.
2. Mann, S., Vrij, A., and Bull, R. (2004) 'Detecting true lies: Police officers' ability to detect deceit'. *Journal of Applied Psychology* 89(1), pp. 137–49.
3. Nichols, R. G., and Stevens, L. A. (1957) *Are You Listening?* New York: McGraw Hill.
4. DePaulo, B. M., Lindsay, J. J., Malone, B. E., et al. (2003) 'Cues to Deception'. *Psychological Bulletin* 129(1), pp. 74–118.
5. Schweitzer, M. E., and Croson, R. (1999) 'Curtailing deception: The impact of direct questions on lies and

omissions'. *International Journal of Conflict Management* 10(3), pp. 225–48.
6. DePaulo, B. M., and Kashy, D. A. (1998) 'Everyday lies in close and casual relationships'. *Journal of Personality and Social Psychology* 74(1), pp. 63–79. 10.1037//0022-3514.74.1.63.
7. Lewis, M., and Saarni, C. (eds.) (1993) *Lying and Deception in Everyday Life*. New York: Guilford Press.
8. Weiss, B., and Feldman, R. S. (2006) 'Looking good and lying to do it: Deception as an impression management strategy in job interviews'. *Journal of Applied Social Psychology* 36(4), pp. 1070–86. https://doi.org/10.1111/j.0021-9029.2006.00055.x
9. These goals and intentions are known as an Illocutionary Speech Act in linguistics. There are five major categories of these: Assertives: the speaker is naming and stating things or facts; Directives: these make the addressee do something for the speaker so cover requests and commands; Expressives: these describe the emotional state of the speaker like thanking and apologising; Commissives: these commit the speaker to doing something in the future such as promises and threats; Declaratives: these change the state of the world in some way like declaring someone under arrest or firing someone. Searle, J. R. (1979) *Expression and Meaning: Studies in the Theories of Speech Acts*. Cambridge: Cambridge University Press.
10. Erat, S., and Gneezy, U. (2012) 'White lies'. *Management Science* 58(4), pp. 723–33.

11. p. 108 of Levin, E. E., and Schweitzer, M. E. (2014) 'Are liars ethical? On the tension between benevolence and honesty'. *Journal of Experimental Social Psychology* 53, pp. 107–17. http://dx.doi.org/10.1016/j.jesp.2014.03.005
12. Hancock, K., Clayton, J. M., Parker, S. M., Wal der, S., Butow, P. N., Carrick, S. et al. (2007) 'Truth-telling in discussing prognosis in advanced life-limiting illnesses: A systematic review'. *Palliative Medicine* 21(6), pp. 507–17.
13. Levin, E. E., and Schweitzer, M. E. (2014) 'Are liars ethical? On the tension between benevolence and honesty'. *Journal of Experimental Social Psychology* 53, pp. 107–17. http://dx.doi.org/10.1016/j.jesp.2014.03.005
14. Greuel, L. (1992) 'Police officers' beliefs about cues associated with deception in rape cases', in Lösel, F., Bender, D., and Bliesener, T. (eds.), *Psychology and the Law: International Perspectives* (pp. 234–9). Berlin: de Gruyter. Kaufmann, G., Drevland, G. C., Wessel, E., Overskeid, G., and Magnussen, S. (2003) 'The importance of being earnest: Displayed emotions and witness credibility'. *Applied Cognitive Psychology* 17(1), pp. 21–34.
15. Gilbert, D. T., Krull, D. S., and Malone, P. S. (1990) 'Unbelieving the unbelievable: Some problems in the rejection of false information'. *Journal of Personality and Social Psychology* 59(4), pp. 601–13.
16. Levine, T. R., Park, H. S., and McCornack, S. A. (1999) 'Accuracy in detecting truths and lies: Documenting the "veracity effect"'. *Communication Monographs* 66(2), pp. 125–44. Gilbert, D. T., Krull, D. S., and Malone, P. S.

(1990) 'Unbelieving the unbelievable: Some problems in the rejection of false information'. *Journal of Personality and Social Psychology* 59(4), pp. 601–13.
17. Posner, M. I. (1980) 'Orienting of attention'. *Quarterly Journal of Experimental Psychology* 32(1), pp. 3–25.
18. Simons, D. J., and Chabris, C. F. (1999) 'Gorillas in our midst: Sustained inattentional blindness for dynamic events'. *Perception* 28(9), pp. 1059–74.
19. Rogers, T., and Norton, M. I. (2011) 'The artful dodger: Answering the wrong question the right way'. *Journal of Experimental Psychology: Applied* 17(2), pp. 139–47.
20. p. 140, Rogers, T., and Norton, M. I. (2011) 'The artful dodger: Answering the wrong question the right way'. *Journal of Experimental Psychology: Applied* 17(2), pp. 139–47.
21. Anthony Weiner interview with Wolf Blitzer, 1 June 2011. https://www.youtube.com/watch?v=xeiIOzFPsqg
22. Cuddy, A. J. C., Fiske, S. T., and Glick, P. (2008) 'Warmth and competence as universal dimensions of social perception: The Stereotype Content Model and BIAS Map', in Zanna, M. P. (ed.), *Advances in Experimental Social Psychology*, vol. 40. New York: Academic Press, pp. 61–149.
23. Rogers, T., and Norton, M. I. (2011) 'The artful dodger: Answering the wrong question the right way'. *Journal of Experimental Psychology: Applied* 17(2), pp. 139–47.
24. Publications and conferences are now appearing which discuss this manipulation, and there are now many internet sites related to its manifestation and

identification, sadly even some which give instructions on how to gaslight others.

25. Stern, R. (2007) *The Gaslight Effect: How to spot and survive the hidden manipulation others use to control your life.* New York: Morgan Read Books.
26. Nazzi, T., Jusczyk, P. W., and Johnson, E. K. (2000) 'Language discrimination by English-learning 5-month-olds: Effects of rhythm and familiarity'. *Journal of Memory and Language* 43(1), 1–19. https://doi.org/10.1006/jmla.2000.2698
27. Flege, J. E. (1984) 'The detection of French accent by American listeners'. *The Journal of the Acoustical Society of America* 76(3), pp. 692–707. https://doi.org/10.1121/1.391256
28. Tsurutani, C., and Selvanathan, E. (2013) 'Influence of generational cohort and experience with non-native speakers on evaluation of speakers with foreign-accented speech'. *International Journal of the Sociology of Language* 2013(224), pp. 43–62. https://doi.org/10.1515/ijsl-2013-0055
29. Castillo P. A., Tyson G., and Mallard D. (2014) 'An investigation of accuracy and bias in cross-cultural lie detection'. *Applied Psychology in Criminal Justice* 10(1), pp. 66–82.
30. Lev-Ari, S., and Keysar, B. (2010) 'Why don't we believe non-native speakers? The influence of accent on credibility'. *Journal of Experimental Social Psychology* 46(6), pp. 1093–6. https://doi.org/10.1016/j.jesp.2010.05.025
31. Romero-Rivas, C., Morgan, C., and Collier, T. (2022) 'Accentism on trial: Categorization/stereotyping

and implicit biases predict harsher sentences for foreign-accented defendants'. *Journal of Language and Social Psychology* 41(2), pp. 191–208. https://doi.org/10.1177/0261927X211022785

32. Kang, O., Vo, S., and Moran, M. K. (2016) 'Perceptual judgments of accented speech by listeners from different first language backgrounds'. *The Electronic Journal for Teaching English as a Second Language* 20(1), pp. 1–24.

33. Akehurst, L., Arnhold, A., Figueiredo, I., Turtle, S., and Leach, A.-M. (2018) 'Investigating deception in second language speakers: Interviewee and assessor perspectives'. *Legal and Criminological Psychology* 23(2), pp. 230–51. https://doi.org/10.1111/lcrp.12127

34. Lev-Ari, S., and Keysar, B. (2010) 'Why don't we believe non-native speakers? The influence of accent on credibility'. *Journal of Experimental Social Psychology* 46(6), pp. 1093–6.

35. Unkelbach, C. (2007) 'Reversing the truth effect: Learning the interpretation of processing fluency in judgments of truth'. *Journal of Experimental Psychology: Learning, Memory, and Cognition* 33(1), pp. 219–30. https://doi.org/10.1037/0278-7393.33.1.219

36. Da Silva, C. S., and Leach, A.-M. (2013) 'Detecting deception in second-language speakers'. *Legal and Criminological Psychology* 18(1), pp. 115–27.

37. Duranti, A., and Brenneis, D. (1986) 'The audience as co-author'. *Text* 6(3), pp. 239–47.

38. Akehurst, L., Arnhold, A., Figueiredo, I., Turtle, S., and Leach, A.-M. (2018) 'Investigating deception in second

language speakers: Interviewee and assessor perspectives'. *Legal and Criminological Psychology* 23(2), pp. 230–51. https://doi.org/10.1111/lcrp.12127
39. http://abcnews.go.com/Politics/video/flashback-john-edwards-denies-affair-5545530
40. https://www.standard.co.uk/news/crime/man-accused-of-murdering-and-cutting-up-pc-he-met-on-grindr-im-a-nice-guy-a3383171.html
41. O'Sullivan, M. (2003) 'The fundamental attribution error in detecting deception: The boy-who-cried-wolf effect'. *Personality and Social Psychology Bulletin* 29(10), pp. 1316–27.
42. Harris, M. J., and Garris, C. P. (2008) 'You never get a second chance to make a first impression: Behavioral consequences of first impressions', in Ambady, N., and Skowronski, J. J. (eds.), *First Impressions* (pp. 147–68). New York, NY, US: Guilford Press.
43. Mileva, M., Tompkinson, J., Watt, D., and Burton, A. M. (2020) 'The role of face and voice cues in predicting the outcome of student representative elections'. *Personality and Social Psychology Bulletin* 46(4), pp. 617–25. https://doi.org/10.1177/0146167219867965
44. Downes, A. C., and Lyons, P. M. (1991) 'Natural observations of the links between attractiveness and initial legal judgments'. *Personality and Social Psychology Bulletin* 17(5), pp. 541–47.
45. Meibauer, J. (2007) 'Lying and falsely implicating', in Mecke, J. (ed.), *Cultures of Lying: Theories and Practice of*

*Lying in Society, Literature, and Film*. Galda + Wilch Verlag: Glienicke/Berlin. pp. 79–114.
46. *Oxford Dictionary of English* (online edition 2015).
47. 'Auguries of Innocence' in Gilchrist, A. (1863) *A Life of William Blake*. London: Macmillan & Co.
48. Rogers, T., Zeckhauser, R., Gino, F., Norton, M. I., and Schweitzer, M. E. (2017) 'Artful paltering: The risks and rewards of using truthful statements to mislead others'. *Journal of Personality and Social Psychology* 112(3), pp. 456–73.
49. Loftus, E. F. (2005) 'Planting misinformation in the human mind: A 30-year investigation of the malleability of memory'. *Learning & Memory* 12(4), pp. 361–6.
50. Bartlett, F. C. (1932) *Remembering: A study in experimental and social psychology*. Cambridge: Cambridge University Press.
51. Granhag, P. A., Strömwall, L. A., and Jonsson, A.-C. (2003) 'Partners in crime: How liars in collusion betray themselves'. *Journal of Applied Social Psychology* 33(4), pp. 848–68.
52. O'Keefe, A., McCarthy, M., and Carter, R. (2007) *From Corpus to Classroom*. Cambridge University Press, Cambridge.
53. Tsui, A. B. M. (1991) 'The pragmatic functions of *I don't know*'. *Text – Interdisciplinary Journal for the Study of Discourse* 11(4), pp. 607–22.
54. Aijmer, K. (2009) 'So er I just sort I dunno I think it's just because . . .—a corpus study of I don't know and dunno in learners' spoken English'. *Language and Computers* 68(1), pp. 151–68.

55. Vrij, A., Granhag, P. A., Ashkenazi, T., Ganis, G., Leal, S., and Fisher, R. P. (2022) 'Verbal lie detection: Its past, present and future'. *Brain Sciences* 12(12), 1644.
56. Debey, E., De Schryver, M., Logan, G. D., Suchotzki, K., and Verschuere, B. (2015) 'From junior to senior Pinocchio: A cross-sectional lifespan investigation of deception'. *Acta Psychologica* 160, pp. 58–68.
57. Vrij, A., Mann, S., Kristen, S., and Fisher, R. P. (2007) 'Cues to deception and ability to detect lies as a function of police interview styles'. *Law and Human Behavior* 31(5), pp. 499–518.
58. Vrij, A., Mann, S. A., Fisher, R. P., Leal, S., Milne, R., and Bull, R. (2008) 'Increasing cognitive load to facilitate lie detection: The benefit of recalling an event in reverse order'. *Law and Human Behavior* 32(3), pp. 253–65.
59. http://www.mirror.co.uk/news/uk-news/becky-watts-murder-trial-watch-6619890
60. McQuaid, S. M., Woodworth, M., Hutton, E. L., Porter, S., and ten Brinke, L. (2015) 'Automated insights: Verbal cues to deception in real-life high-stakes lies'. *Psychology, Crime & Law* 21(7), pp. 617–31.
61. Walczyk, J. J., Roper, K. S., Seemann, E., and Humphrey, A. M. (2003) 'Cognitive mechanisms underlying lying to questions: Response time as a cue to deception'. *Applied Cognitive Psychology* 17(7), pp. 755–74.
62. Lewandowsky, S., Ecker, U. K. H., Seifert, C. M., Schwarz, N., and Cook, J. (2012) 'Misinformation and its

correction: Continued influence and successful debiasing'. *Psychological Science in the Public Interest* 13(3), pp. 106–31.

## CONCLUSION

1. For a review see Vrij, A. (2004) 'Why professionals fail to catch liars and how they can improve'. *Legal and Criminological Psychology* 9(2), pp. 159–81.
2. Vrij, A., and Semin, G. R. (1996) 'Lie experts' beliefs about nonverbal indicators of deception'. *Journal of Nonverbal Behavior* 20(1), pp. 65–80.
3. Tausczik, Y. R., and Pennebaker, J. W. (2010) 'The psychological meaning of words: LIWC and computerized text analysis methods'. *Journal of Language and Social Psychology* 29(1), pp. 24–54.

Dr Kirsty King is a lecturer in communication at University College London. She holds a PhD in linguistics (University of London) and an Advanced Diploma in forensic linguistics, and has lectured in linguistics for over twenty years at the University of London. She is a member of the International Association of Forensic Linguists and a committee member of the Anthropology and Language Committee of the Royal Anthropological Institute. She lives in London.